I Bought
a House
on Gratitude
Street

Gratitude — love with a memory.

J. ELLSWORTH KALAS

I Bought a House on Gratitude Street

And Other Insights on the Good Life

Abingdon Press
Nashville

I BOUGHT A HOUSE ON GRATITUDE STREET
AND OTHER INSIGHTS ON THE GOOD LIFE

Copyright © 2011 by Abingdon Press

Libary of Congress Cataloging-in-Publication Data

Kalas, J. Ellsworth, 1923-
  I bought a house on Gratitude Street : and other insights on the good life / J. Ellsworth Kalas.
      p. cm.
  ISBN 978-1-4267-1461-0 (pbk. : alk. paper)
  1. Christian life—Methodist authors.   I. Title.
  BV4501.3.K35 2011
  248.4'87—dc22

                                                              2010054430

11 12 13 14 15 16 17 18 19 20—10 9 8 7 6 5 4 3 2 1

MANUFACTURED IN THE UNITED STATES OF AMERICA

Contents

CONTENTS

INTRODUCTION TO
GRATITUDE STREET

I am blessed in having been on this earth long enough to accumulate assorted pieces of daily wisdom. Some of these insights have come to me by my seeking, some have been shared with me by people of wider experience, and some have been thrust upon me by my mistakes. I am grateful, however, regardless of the method of delivery.

Let me hasten to say that though so much wisdom has come my way, I don't always live up to it. This confession itself demonstrates how wise I've become: I know enough to make an apology before one is demanded of me. I am recommending the wisdom of these lessons, not my infallibility.

These insights won't save your soul, but they may help you to keep saved—and they will almost surely make it easier for others around you to live happily. These life observations have come to me from people both great and small—by our world's standards, more of the latter than of the former. Some people have conveyed their lessons directly and intentionally, while others have left them in print, never knowing that I would be an eventual beneficiary. But a number of the lessons have crept up on me unawares, without my being on a conscious quest for improvement. This doesn't contradict my saying a moment ago that some of these insights have come by my seeking. It's just that what I've gotten hasn't always been what I was seeking. I've often stumbled upon the lovely when I was only looking for the nice.

These little lessons include living with our past and taking conquest of our future. They have to do with getting along with others, often by way of getting along with ourselves. They are as immediate as falling asleep at night and as long-range as bringing in the kingdom of God. They include matters of friendship and prayer and sin and success.

I don't have a scripture text for each chapter, but I've tried to be sure that what I've written is scripturally sound. As I've said at other times and places, I read through the Bible for the first time when I was eleven years old, and I have read the Bible in its entirety scores of times since then, in almost every English translation, from the King James to the Common English Bible. As a result, whatever ideas or theories come to me have almost surely passed through the prism of the Book that has blessed all of my life. If you consider this a weakness in me, I will consider your judgment a compliment. I am unapologetically a child of the Bible, and my only regret is in the limits of my understanding and in my failures of living up to what the Bible has taught me.

We will begin this journey with my home on Gratitude Street. You may wonder why I haven't chosen that greatest of biblical words, *love*. Well, in a sense I have. Gratitude is love applied. It is, as I say in the opening chapter, love with a memory. And gratitude nurtures such other virtues as humility and joy. But I'm getting ahead of myself. I invite you to join me now in the journey that follows.

With love—and gratitude,
J. Ellsworth Kalas

CHAPTER 1

I Bought a House on Gratitude Street

Some years ago I bought a house on Gratitude Street. I can't say when I made the purchase, because getting this house wasn't like signing a conventional contract. I seemed simply to ease into ownership, until I had a kind of squatter's rights mentality about the property and realized that now it was my own. But of this I am absolutely sure, that I never intend, ever again, to live anywhere else.

Before I go further I want to underline that I did, indeed, *buy* this house. Yet at the same time I've used the right word when I speak of "squatter's rights." The property was empty and I made it mine by building there, by cultivating the property, and by keeping it up. And I'm quite sure that if I ever allow the property to run down or the yard to be covered with weeds, I will lose my rights.

You can be sure that I never intend to let that happen. Because of course the longer I live here the more I love the place and the more I have invested in it. My only regret is the regret all of us have after we have established ourselves in a grand and lovely decision: I wonder why I didn't make the decision earlier.

In truth, I wasn't ready years ago. Most of us have to live a while in order to accumulate the wherewithal to buy a property, and goodness knows I've needed time to get my spiritual and emotional resources to the place where I could make a purchase like this one. People who buy a physical property usually need time to accumulate a down payment. But the skills needed to save tens of thousands of dollars are nothing compared with the insight, the self-knowledge, and the discipline that we need if we're to buy a house on Gratitude Street. A purchase on Gratitude Street involves a peculiar kind of spiritual enlightenment—the kind of enlightenment that, at least for most of us, involves maturity. Mind you, I'm not making a case for age. Some people buy a house on this street while they're still relatively young. I wasn't that perceptive. On the other hand, most people never move into the neighborhood, not even in their retirement years. I still insist, however, that getting this property is a matter of maturity, whatever the age—specifically, of coming to a place where we're able to stand the shock of knowing some crucial facts about ourselves.

The biggest of which is this: that essentially everything we have is a gift. If you insist on holding to the conviction that you're a self-made person, you'll never buy property on Gratitude Street. That's where maturity comes in. Because maturity involves humility and humility is very hard to come by. Often it comes to us only by way of a fair number of defeats. And the defeats themselves are not enough; we must come to the place where we can admit our role in the defeat, in some cases even to acknowledge that the defeat or failure was primarily our own doing—none of this, "If it hadn't been for so-and-so, I wouldn't have made such a mess." We must come to the place where we stop looking for others to blame.

I'm not suggesting that everything that goes wrong in our lives is our own fault. Usually more than one person is required if we're to get a full-scale mess. But it's always difficult to see our personal role in our failures. At the same time it's crucially important to see at what points the fault is our own, since we can't do much about the part others have played in our failures. It's foolish to waste our time looking for co-conspirators in our misfortunes when we can't do anything to remedy the errors or evil intentions of others. Rather, recognize the measure of our responsibility in the pain we've suffered, do what we can to remedy it or to see that it doesn't happen again, and move on. This calls for both self-knowledge and humility.

And then we must move to the place where we can see what others have done to make our lives better. Some are big and some are small. The high school teacher who was my debate coach is *big*. I can never be grateful enough for the demanding way he compelled me to believe in excellence—a concept difficult for a sixteen-year-old but that F. O. Racker drilled deep into my soul. Likewise, I owe a debt, but a smaller one, to school friends who taught me little lessons along the way that rubbed off some of my rough edges—and while my debt to each one is relatively small, the cumulative effect is very large. I owe a large debt to those individuals who spoke key words at just the right time—and a smaller debt to those persons who prepared the soil of my soul for the key word by speaking preparatory words at less sensitive moments in my journey.

I sometimes think that deprivation provides especially good soil for feelings of gratitude. During my growing-up years I had very few economic, educational, or social advantages, so any favor that came my way made a deep impression. Some of my school friends (though not those in my geographical neighborhood) had professional parents who were college graduates. The only college graduates I knew were my schoolteachers and my minister. I wonder who first planted in my soul the idea that someday I might go to college. How was it that I became so enthralled with the idea of college that I devoured boys' novels about prep school and college life? I will never know who planted that mustard seed of a dream in my soul, but it was a seed that grew into a sturdy plant so that all of the winds of poverty and disparagement couldn't uproot it. I am grateful beyond expression to that unknown, unremembered person or persons who told me I should and could go to college someday.

But deprivation alone won't make one grateful. Some use it as an excuse for continued failure and disappointment. And when we rise above deprivation, it can easily make us small and mean inside so that after gaining a diploma or some other measure of success we boast that we've done it ourselves, and that anyone else could do the same if only they'd work as hard as we did. I am impressed, in another way, by people who have grown up in the contours of privilege, where life's favors are commonplace and easily taken for granted, but who nevertheless have a spirit of gratitude. Gratitude by no means depends on circumstances alone, either positive or negative.

Sometimes a particular experience makes the issue of gratitude so clear that we can almost date it. I remember a friend of my teenage years who, though he was only in his midtwenties, had spent two years in a tubercular sanatorium, at times on the edge of death. He said one day as he was sipping a glass of water at a kitchen sink, "I never drink a glass of water—never!—without thanking God that I'm alive. Drinking water reminds me how close I was to death." The water wasn't Perrier. It wasn't even blessed by an ice cube. Just a glass of lukewarm water from a 1940s kitchen spigot, but an impetus to gratitude.

There's no doubt but that gratitude is helped by contrast and comparison. I'm grateful for an operating automobile because I've had some that were not dependable. I'm thankful for emergency roadside service because at an earlier time in my life I jacked up an automobile many times to change flat tires. I am grateful for sunshine because I've known rain, for friendship because I've experienced loneliness, for laughter because I've cried. These days, when I have enough, I remember with gratitude the times when I had nothing. In truth, I feel sorry for some of my acquaintances who don't know when they have enough. This, in itself, is a tragic poverty.

Gratitude that is not expressed is meaningless. Gratitude is not complete if it is simply a feeling within one's bosom. Unfortunately, however, we often leave gratitude in that unfinished state. This is because gratitude itself is such a warm and fuzzy feeling that we think the feeling is itself the essence of gratitude when in truth the feeling is just the beginning. To feel thankful and to do nothing about it, to express our thanks to no one, forces gratitude into a stillbirth.

Gratitude must have an outlet. Gratitude unexpressed is gratitude unfulfilled, and it will never buy a house on Gratitude Street.

Gratitude can begin at the simplest level, but it eventually needs a rather profound base. Our parents were right when they insisted, "Johnny, say thank you to the nice lady." Unfortunately, some allow their thank-you to stop at this perfunctory level, with no feeling accompanying the words. Such a thank-you becomes an insult rather than a social favor. An insincere thank-you or a thoughtless one is an oxymoron because the basic ingredient in "thank you" is the feeling of gratitude. But of course it is much easier to teach children a phrase than to teach them an attitude. The attitude is caught from an atmosphere lived out by others and then undergirded by the knowledge that our lives are made rich every day, every hour, by things others living and dead have done and are doing for us.

So we recognize these favors and we give thanks. Someone invites us to go through a door first: we're grateful and we show it. At a moment of traffic congestion a driver waves us ahead and in gratitude we wave a thank-you. We feel better for that driver's kindness, and still better for letting him or her know that we're grateful. The person who accepts such kindnesses without acknowledgement has stopped the flow of goodness and made the world smaller. Why do some people find it hard to confess that their day has been made easier by another person's generosity? Are any of us so important that we think we deserve an advanced place in line? How lovely that someone would let us in!

So, too, with the occasions for which we might argue that we owe no thanks. Should we thank the person who serves us at the checkout line? Some would reason that these persons are paid to take care of us, and indeed to do so pleasantly—and occasionally some of them aren't pleasant. Then why thank them? My answer: primarily because I'm glad for their service, no matter that they are paid to do it, and I am especially grateful when they do it graciously. But more than that, I have felt ever since moving to Gratitude Street that it is my privilege to extend the mood of the street on which I live. And I continue to marvel at the change that so often happens when I act with goodwill in these passing encounters. The airport attendant who is receiving the boarding pass looks up and smiles when I say with a smile, "Thank you!"—and the attendant often adds, "Have a good trip!" The checkout person is startled by goodwill. Not always, mind you. I'm a realist and a truthful man, so I acknowledge that some people are so imprisoned by their own problems that they seem to reject goodwill. No matter! What have I lost? Gratitude is its own reward.

It is also important to express gratitude to those with whom we have the closest association, especially those in our own household. The commonplace tasks of each day cease to be commonplace if we see them with gratitude. They receive the stature of honor they deserve. The tasks that every household member performs should not lose their value simply because they are always there. Sad to say, some persons in a family, a workplace, or a dormitory only get recognized when they miss their routine assignment—and then with a sharp word. Gratitude is a better way, and it improves one's own residence on Gratitude Street.

As gratitude becomes a way of life, we become conscious of reasons for gratitude that never occurred to us before. People and deeds come to mind, prompting us to make a telephone call, send an e-mail, or write a note. Do it! Some of these promptings come from a matter from last week or last month, and some come—quite unbidden—from half a lifetime ago. In such instances from the past, we often don't know if the person is still living and, if so, where to find them—and then we're grateful for the wonders of the world of the Internet, to assist our search. Often the "late" word of thanks has gained worth by the passage of time because the recipient is astonished to be remembered after so long.

But what of the feeling of gratitude that is too late? The person for whom we feel thankful is long dead or proves to be quite out of reach. What then?

I deal with this question every year, on schedule. I return to my hometown each summer, to see the two or three friends who still live there, but mostly to visit with my friendly ghosts. I go to the old neighborhoods, the schools I attended, the public libraries that graced my life and the churches that marked my spiritual pilgrimage, and I thank God for all the beautiful people I've known. I'm not sure how well I thanked them long ago; teenage boys are not always eloquent in expressing their gratitude. Do they hear me now, those long-ago friends, schoolteachers, ministers and Sunday school teachers? I don't know. I'm not enough of a metaphysician to have an explanation, and I find no clear words in the Scriptures. But this I know: I need to tell them. Gratitude compels me to speak their names, to recall the occasions, sometimes to apologize for my shortcomings in our relationships, and always to thank God for the divine kindness in allowing such special people to enter my life.

Always and increasingly I thank God. I need God for salvation and for a sense of forgiveness and for strength and insight to live the right kind of life; but above all, I need God as the recipient of my gratitude. I feel sad when I think of that remarkable writer from the early twentieth century, Katherine Mansfield, who insisted that she couldn't believe in a personal God—and from that posture wrote on an especially glorious day, "If only one could make some small grasshoppery sound of praise to *someone*—thanks to *some-one*. But who?"[1]

I am grateful for the *Who*, for God to whom I can give thanks. I am grateful not only to have a divine heart waiting to hear my gratitude, but also because so much of my gratitude is complex and interwoven. I try to determine the place some individual, living or dead, or some experience has played in my life and find that individuals and experiences interweave and intersect in such intricate beauty (and for me, sometimes, confusion) that I too fumble for a "small grasshoppery sound"—but with unfettered gratitude to God, who understands my feeling and who finds pleasure in my incoherence.

I have learned never to leave gratitude to chance. My place on Gratitude Street depends on constant awareness. So each morning, within the first half-hour of the day, I list the three or four matters from the previous day for which I am grateful. Almost always some person is in the list, as well as some event. Some are commonplace parts of everyday life, but somehow have particular significance on the day just past. So I list it. Some people appear on my list often, but for different reasons and with a different contour to their beauty.

And I am specific. It isn't enough to say, "For all my blessings." Name them! "Name them one by one," as a nineteenth-century hymn writer put it. Was yesterday a perfect fall day? Then give some particulars to the word of thanks. Was lunch special? Say why. Did you pass safely through a hard place? Recall it, and be glad.

Several years ago, on a Thanksgiving Eve when Mrs. Kalas and I couldn't find a worship service to attend, we made our own. The practice has blessed us ever since. We sing or recite the words to some of the loveliest hymns of thanksgiving, then with eyes closed and with hearts open, we begin alternately to give thanks—usually for one item at a time, sometimes with only a phrase and at others with a whole paragraph, but never for long, because what one of us says evokes a thought from the other and the flow of gratitude needs immediate expression. In this exercise we leave no room for a petition; it is time for thanks and for thanks alone. Every year we are astonished at the matters that come to mind, astonished at all the goodness that attends our lives, goodness that sometimes we hadn't recognized when it happened, and goodness that in retrospect is lovelier than ever.

I have come to realize that while love is wonderful, gratitude has a place all by itself, because gratitude is love with a memory. And of course gratitude allows no place for repayment because gratitude needs no reward. The heart knows that it is privilege enough to live one's life on Gratitude Street.

NOTE

1. Vincent O'Sullivan and Margaret Scott, eds., *The Collected Letters of Katherine Mansfield,* vol. 4 (Oxford: Oxford University Press, 1996), 252.

CHAPTER 2

Keep Confessed Up

Many of life's most memorable lessons come without our recognizing the lesson until years later. Such lessons come not so much as "aha moments" as an accumulation of experiences, conversations, and reading that add up, we hardly know how, to a special way of looking at life. But some lessons come packaged within a particular conversation or in a specific individual. We remember not only the insight itself, but the person and the circumstances of delivery.

For me, in this instance, it was the summer of 1941. I had been chosen to travel with a male quartet, four men ages eighteen to twenty-nine who were serving as goodwill ambassadors for a small religious school. America was on the precipice of entry into World War II that summer, but most people were avoiding the thought, including the four of us. We knew our assignment, and we loved it. We were scheduled to travel through fifteen states in fifteen weeks, from Missouri to Minnesota and from Pennsylvania to Wyoming, singing in churches, usually in one-night stands. But when we arrived in Terre Haute, Indiana, it was to spend the whole weekend there, and since there was no service on Saturday evening, Saturday came as a lovely, carefree day, with time to talk and to listen.

So it was that I listened to Brother Williamson. The title doesn't mean that he was a monk or a member of some religious order, but a Pentecostal preacher. In that simpler, gentler time, we often addressed older spiritual leaders of recognized quality as Brother or Sister and often didn't know their given name. I was eighteen and ready to be instructed, and Brother Williamson was ready to talk. So on a hot summer afternoon I plied this man with questions about life and God and service to humanity. As he talked and I listened, I wanted some portable memory of our visit, so I asked him to write in the back of my Bible: something I had never before asked anyone to do and have never asked since.

Most of what he wrote was predictable—that I should read my Bible daily and pray first thing in the morning. But there was another sentence: *Keep confessed up.*

I wish I had always done so. If I had, I wouldn't have repeated some sins, and I would have avoided some unwise and self-destructive courses. Mind you, I thought of the rule often, but as with many elements of worthwhile knowledge I didn't always think of it when I needed the reminder the most. Yet even though I haven't managed one hundred percent compliance with Brother Williamson's rule, it has blessed my life more than I can reasonably estimate.

The ancient Hebrews, wise as they were, built the principle of scheduled repentance into their calendar. As a nation, they confessed their sins annually, by way of the Day of Atonement. There was nothing incidental or haphazard about this; it was a set day in the year and the nation made its confession before God whether or not they thought it necessary. Mind you, the Hebrew Scriptures also had rather detailed provisions for *individual, personal* confession at any time during the year, but the Day of Atonement was a time of national repentance, a time for spiritual and emotional housecleaning. As such it was not only structured but quite dramatic in some of its ritual.

I'm sure that the power and majesty and drama of this ritual helped Israel to know the seriousness of repentance. I think this mood from the Day of Repentance carried forward in at least a measure in the individual's attitude toward sin and repentance. Not for everyone, obviously, and not for every infraction of the divine-human relationship, but there was no doubt a divine fallout from the Day of Atonement that left its impress on the lives of many—perhaps a majority—of sensitive Israelites.

I speak as an outsider, but I suspect that Roman Catholicism lost some of its authority as an agent of repentance with the downplaying of the confessional in more recent years. True, the confessional was treated casually by casual Catholics, and was probably made a fruitless burden by those who were overly scrupulous, perhaps sometimes pathologically so, persons who found some peculiar satisfaction in the sense of guilt. But for those who were ready to face themselves seriously in the confessional, the regular opportunity for repentance was both spiritually and psychologically restorative, as it still is for those who use it properly.

We Protestants are generally weak in providing a venue for confession of sin. In my earlier years as a pastor, most liturgical churches included a time for confession of sins, sometimes primarily through a period of silence before God and others by way of a written prayer. But I find that very few rituals of worship still include a place for confession of sins. I know full well that such confessions usually had a quality of rote and that probably only a few worshipers thought about what they were saying—unless, perhaps, to feel that the particulars of the confession didn't really apply to them. Nevertheless, I feel we've lost something by omitting such an action from our worship.

The celebration of Holy Communion still provides this opportunity in many churches. The invitation to commune is extended specifically to those "who earnestly repent of their sin," and the prayer that follows is one of confession. The intention is altogether right, and the occasion—the accepting of the body and blood of Christ—is the ultimate setting. But do we feel it and mean it? I'm not sure.

Some have a special vehicle for confession by participating in an accountability group. Such groups usually have a special time for candid discussion of each person's standing before God, with acknowledgement to one another of any ways in which there has been a violation of their relationship before God and their pledge to one another. This practice sustains many believers. Having made a pledge to others brings clarity and intention to self-examination that very possibly wouldn't exist if members of the group were going their own private way in their devotional lives.

Samuel Johnson, the eminent English literary figure of the eighteenth century, was a great soul in many ways, especially in his practice of confession. Among secular saints, he may have done as well as anyone in fulfilling Brother Williamson's rule. Johnson sought to "keep confessed up." His written prayers demonstrate that fact. He made particular use of his birthday and of New Year's Day to make confession. He considered both of these days as an opportunity to make a new start, and he was wise enough—with the wisdom of true saintliness—to know that a new start must begin with taking care of old business. For Johnson, the old business was confession of sin.

Like most of us, Samuel Johnson had a besetting sin. He expressed his in a variety of words (after all, he produced the first English dictionary!)—words like *sloth, idleness, folly, negligence.* He repented for "time lost," time "lost in idleness," and of "the time misspent," while also praying to "improve the time." Thus, on his fifty-seventh birthday in 1766, "enable me so to spend my remaining days, that, by performing thy will, I may promote thy glory." On his seventieth birthday he rejoiced that his life had been prolonged "to the common age of Man," and appealed: "and accept, O Lord, the remains of a misspent life, that when Thou shalt call me to another state, I may be received to everlasting happiness, for the sake of Jesus Christ our Lord."

Johnson's struggle had to do with his sociability. He loved to eat and talk with friends far into the night, which then caused him to sleep late in the morning; and since he supported himself by his writing, he was essentially the sole arbiter of his time.

Anyone who has read Boswell's classic biography of Dr. Johnson knows that a vast number of Johnson's aphorisms came to birth in those late-night visits, which may make us glad that the good man never won the victory over his nocturnal habits. His "sloth" and "time misspent" has filled pages in the various dictionaries of quotations. No matter; Johnson felt that he would have been a much more productive worker if he had put himself under the discipline of more regular hours.

So of what value was Dr. Johnson's constant confessing? Was it nothing more than a good man's method of self-chastising? Would he have done better, if counselors had been available in his day, to have sought such professional help rather than simply confessing his sins year after year? I have no desire to pass judgment on Samuel Johnson, who is something of a hero to me. His besetting sin doesn't happen to be mine, which makes me all the more careful about judging him. At the least, I submit that he would probably have been far more slothful if it were not for the sense of sin and his profound willingness to bring his weakness to God.

I submit also that by his confessing Johnson acquired a purity of heart and a graciousness of spirit which made him a better person in the whole body of his character. Deliverance from a particular sin is not the only benefit of our faithfulness in confessing. There is a holy fallout in any true confessing of sin: we are blessed by the posture of submission before God and by the humility that comes with the recognition that we are not paragons for admiration but rather, works in progress—and that we're happy to be in such a process of character development.

All of us, religious or not, are in need of improvement. The greatest of us, the true saints, are the ones most conscious of this need. There's nothing morbid about this, no more than it is morbid to seek to know more, to love friends or family more faithfully, or to have better health practices. Indeed, because of what our moral character does to our physical and social health, nothing is more crucial than the right care of our moral character. And that right care includes recognizing our shortcomings and bringing them before God. There, in the divine presence, we confess our shortcoming and we seek a better way.

But if we don't make such confessions, something in the soul diminishes; indeed, may even grow sour. Nothing is more crucial to growth than the recognition of need. If I have become soft or pudgy or sick in body, mind, human relationships, or things of the spirit, I need to confess my condition to change my ways. But if I am to make an effective change, I will need God's help: thus the importance of confessing to *God*. If I make my confession only to my own soul, my journey to wholeness will be a lonely one, probably marked primarily by self-recrimination and self-despising and by little actual soul improvement.

I mentioned in our earlier discussion on gratitude the poignant words of Katherine Mansfield; she longed for someone to whom she could express her gratitude. We humans have the same profound need when it comes to the matter of confession. I dare to say that confession is as insistent a need in the human psyche as is gratitude. As surely as something in our souls wants to say thank you to "whom it may concern," just as surely something in us wants to say, "I'm sorry." All of us know we fall short of our best potential. Mind you, we need help in upgrading our self-expectations; this is where our best preachers, prophets, and poets enter our story. But all of us know that life deserves better of us than we give, and life continually tells us so until we silence our best voices with the soft music of mediocrity.

But I repeat: we need a Divine Listener for our confessions just as we need such a Listener for our gratitude. Our souls are frustrated with anything less. And the need for God as the object of our confession is even more signifi-

16

cant, if possible, than as the recipient for our gratitude—because when we confess, we need the strength to fulfill the better way that the soul envisions and longs for. To use an old but true term, we need to be *saved*. And salvation is a divine enterprise.

I continue to be fascinated with that great soul, King David of Israel. What a human being! Clearly, he was a compelling figure, the kind of person who evoked deep friendships, as with Jonathan, and a person who while still probably only in his twenties could bring together a group of social ne'er-do-wells and make a freelance army of them. It seems that women adored him, whether as a community hero or as a lover. He could fight giants, write poetry, and run a kingdom. But above all it was said of him that he was a man after God's own heart (Acts 13:22).

What was it that qualified David in such an extraordinary way? Almost every modest student of the Bible knows that David was exceedingly human: he committed adultery, then arranged for the murder of the woman's husband. He could be violent and vengeful and self-seeking. What was his redeeming virtue? This, it seems clear—that he wanted to carry out all of God's wishes, and that when he sinned he had the good sense and the passionate desire to set things right. That is, he knew how to confess.

I don't know if David had a Brother Williamson who told him to "keep confessed up," and I don't know if he had some daily or weekly or monthly ritual, some established pattern for doing business with God. It's clear that he had an open-door policy with the prophet Nathan; perhaps Nathan was his spiritual counselor, perhaps one with whom David discussed the matters of his eternal soul and from whom in return he received insight and probably at times also reproof.

In any event, David knew how to confess to God. The superscription to Psalm 51 describes the psalm as David's prayer after the prophet Nathan had confronted him concerning his sin with Bathsheba, the wife of his army officer

Uriah. It is as passionate an appeal for forgiveness and as penetratingly self-reflective as can be found anywhere. David faces what he has done without offering excuse and without looking for someone who can share the blame.

When faced with our sins, it is quite human to counter with an explanation of our right intentions, or to note that anyone else in a similar situation would probably do the same thing, or to note some extenuating circumstances that made us more vulnerable. There is none of that in David's prayer. His soul scenario is simple: he has sinned, and he wants above all to feel clean again. If that happens, he will seek to help others who are in trouble.

We humans are a spiritually vulnerable lot. When David's son, Solomon, prayed at the dedication of the temple, he observed that "there is no one who does not sin" (1 Kings 8:46). Most of us will confirm Solomon's observation, not only by our study of history and by what we have seen in the lives of others, but also by what we have learned about our own souls. It's essential, therefore, that we learn how to deal with this ultimate human problem.

Some say that there's nothing we can do about the past except to live with it. But the Bible teaches otherwise. We can confess to God (and sometimes, under particular circumstances, to another party). Then we can build on our failure, so that by God's grace our loss becomes a benchmark for a better day.

Let me put it in the simplest, most pragmatic terms. All of us have some garbage in our lives, spiritual-intellectual-social rubbish that we shouldn't allow to accumulate. We need a holy place where some of this rubbish can be recycled—I'll talk about that when I deal with the subject of regrets—and some is simply burned up, with the fire lit by our confession and the flame provided by God's grace.

Brother Williamson had it right. *Keep confessed up.* If we do, we can keep our souls strong and ready for each new day.

CHAPTER 3

Don't Take Yourself Too Seriously

We live in a time when self-esteem is among the most prized of goals. Contemporary parents spend a huge amount of emotional energy making sure that their children think well of themselves, and what's left of their energy in regretting that their own parents didn't give them a comparable foundation of self-regard. I'm not as mean as I sound just now. I like for people to be comfortable with themselves and to enjoy pride in their achievements. Nevertheless, I'm about to offer a severely balancing word in this study of the good life. I've concluded that most of us take ourselves far too seriously, often to the discomfort of those around us; and that the world would be better if we'd get over this self-seriousness at least a little bit.

I could make my point with any number of persons known and unknown. I suspect that you could offer me some examples from within your circle of acquaintances, including perhaps your doctor, your minister, your co-worker, or your college roommate. But I've chosen someone who can't take me to court—a Bible character, the man named Elijah.

Elijah was a prophet in the days of Israel's kings. There is no book of the Bible named for him or his writings, as in the case for instance of Isaiah, Jeremiah, and Amos, but in some ways he is held in greater esteem than these literary prophets. When I make this estimate of Elijah's importance, I'm thinking especially of a key point in Jesus' life. When our Lord took Peter, James, and John to Mount Hebron, it was Elijah and Moses who appeared in the ecstatic moment of transfiguration. Most Bible students feel that Moses was there as representative of the Hebrew Law, the Torah, and that Elijah was symbolic of the prophets. This is remarkable, since we have no record of any sermons, teachings, or prophecies from Elijah. We have record of several very brief speeches, but they're more like challenges than structured presentations, notable especially for their tendentious quality and their disregard for counter-opinions and possible danger.

You may already have sensed that although I intend to use Elijah as a negative example, I like him very much. In truth, he's one of my favorite Bible characters. Yes, and more than that. As I think back on personalities I remember from world history and characters in novels and short stories I've read, Elijah would still be part of the final competition of favorite people. I wish I could have known him, and if heaven provides opportunity for meeting people, as I hope and believe it will, I want early to meet Elijah. I should add, however, that I probably would not have volunteered to be part of his team and I am equally certain he wouldn't have chosen me, but I'd love to have observed him from a safe distance. That is, if there was with Elijah such a thing as a safe distance.

But as truly admirable as Elijah was and as much as he fascinates me, he seems to me to have possessed a dramatic flaw in character. In truth, this is probably one of the reasons he appeals to me. His character flaw is one with which I am personally acquainted, so I take comfort in him. And with Elijah, his flaws—like his virtues—are written in bold type, interspersed with exclamation points, so when he fails, it's never a secret. I think I like that too. Better him than me, I figure.

So here's my counsel for the good life as observed in Elijah and as experienced in my own life: *Don't take yourself too seriously.* Always take God seriously, and at select times take other people and life's circumstances seriously. But go easy on yourself. Be ready to see yourself as the joker in the king's deck.

Now let me tell you about Elijah.

We're not prepared for him when he comes on the biblical scene. It was one of those times when things were bad in the nation of Israel, and if you've read the Bible just a bit you know that when things are bad you can expect that God will be on the search for some man or woman who can meet the challenge. At this particular point in Israel's history they had a king named Ahab, who "did evil in the sight of the LORD more than all who were before him" (1 Kings 16:30). This was no small accomplishment. Israel had had a procession of leaders—Jeroboam, Nadab, Baasha, Zimri and Omri—all of whom the biblical historian evaluates with the same terse line: they did evil in the sight of the Lord. The only king in those years of whom no such report is given was Elah, and this is because he reigned only two years before he was struck down during a drunken stupor. In Israel's World Series of Evil, Ahab outranked all of these who had come before him.

And this was before he married Jezebel. You've probably heard of Jezebel, and maybe you've even heard someone nicknamed Jezebel, but I venture you've never known of someone who registered the name on a birth certificate. She was the daughter of the King of the Sidonians, a nation that "served Baal, and worshiped him" (1 Kings 16:31). Ahab obviously had no religious convictions of his own, so he not only joined his wife in Baal worship, he erected an altar to Baal in a special house he had built for that purpose in Samaria. The biblical historian adds a further word about Ahab: he "did more to provoke the anger of the LORD, the God of Israel, than had all the kings of Israel who were before him" (1 Kings 16:33).

That's when Elijah appears. No fanfare, no roll of drums, not even a brief introductory statement. Just this: "Now Elijah the Tishbite, of Tishbe in Gilead, said to Ahab, 'As the LORD the God of Israel lives, before whom I stand, there shall be neither dew nor rain these years, except by my word' " (1 Kings 17:1). A short sermon, but long on wallop. We don't know anything about Elijah's credentials, his family tree, his training, or his previous experience. It's clear, however, that he's not timid and that the authority of the king impressed him not at all.

A drought follows, and with the drought starvation and a rising mood of political unhappiness. Even before people elected presidents and prime ministers, back in the world of hereditary kings, people expected their leaders to be worth something—particularly, to provide them with a reasonably secure life. Kings didn't have to worry about the next election, but their alternative was no gain: they were in danger of armed revolt and of possible assassination. King Ahab felt that the drought was Elijah's fault; after all, he was the one who predicted it. Indeed, he announced it.

In time, Elijah called for a religious showdown. He called for the king to convene the four hundred fifty prophets of Baal and the four hundred prophets of Asherah to come to Mount Carmel for a Super Bowl of Faith. It wasn't hard to bring together this crowd of prophets because Ahab saw them regularly: they did all "eat at Jezebel's table" (1 Kings 18:19).

Well, as you might have guessed, Elijah won. It was wonderfully dramatic, and he did it with a flourish. With all its money and sound effects Hollywood couldn't touch the power of this scene. Because they don't have Elijah! His courage is fearless, his sarcasm is magnificent, and his certainty of victory is untouchable. It is a bloody victory. I know I shouldn't glory in it, yet I confess that I can't help smiling. I'm always inclined toward the underdog, sometimes even when they're playing my own team, so when I see Elijah winning over the eight hundred fifty false prophets before a packed natural stadium—well, it feels good.

And Elijah wasn't done. Now, without a cloud in the sky and after years of no rain, he prayed until he saw a cloud the size of a person's hand and announced to King Ahab that rain was coming. And it did. It poured.

But when King Ahab reported to Jezebel that Elijah had destroyed her whole clergy corps, she didn't take it kindly. By tomorrow at this time, she said, Elijah will be as dead as my prophets.

Elijah can handle this, of course. When you can win before the assembled nation when the odds against you are 850 to one, you can handle one foreign queen. But Elijah couldn't. For one thing, Jezebel was one tough lady—in a sense, cut out of the same type of cloth as Elijah. Besides, Elijah was tired. Tired even to the point of death. So he sat under a broom tree—a rather dreary little bush, but appropriate to Elijah's mood—and asked God if he might die.

Several factors probably led to Elijah's dreary mood. I suspect that he was flat-out tired—mentally and psychologically from his showdown with Jezebel's prophets and physically from his fierce run alongside King Ahab's chariot—and when weariness hits a certain psychic point the whole pitcher of life can turn sour. I think, too, that careers can sometimes have a kind of postpartum psychosis: after waiting at length for a greatly desired outcome, there can be a dramatic letdown when the outcome is fulfilled. Elijah had waited for many years to meet the prophets of Baal and Ashtoreth in open conflict; now he had done so, and had won—and now, what worlds were left to conquer? So when Queen Jezebel sent her threat, Elijah decided to turn in his uniform and leave the team.

But as I see it, the biggest issue was this: Elijah had come to take himself too seriously.

Mind you, he had good reason to do so. Many of us who have succumbed to the same problem have a poor case for drawing the spotlight on ourselves, but Elijah was as justified as anyone has a right to be. It was he who delivered the message of judgment to King Ahab, and it appears he did so without complaint. It was he who stood alone in the face of all the pagan priests, and it was he who dared to tell Ahab that rain was coming, after years of drought.

But with it all, somehow Elijah had come to feel unappreciated. Or at the least, underappreciated. He got the feeling that God didn't realize how faithful he had been, and how important he was to the divine enterprise. Elijah's pain came from what he perceived to be his poor standing before God. Political leaders feel it when the polls turn against them, a parent when children express their independence or their seeming indifference, an employee at the end of the workweek (possibly just when the employee's employer is having the same feeling). Which is to say, we're all very susceptible to the feeling that we aren't appreciated. Elijah said, "I have been very zealous for the LORD.... I alone am left..." (1 Kings 19:10, 14).

How do we get in this state of mind? It usually begins at a very admirable place, our dedication. Every virtue has its back side; such is the nature of sin. Self-importance is the back side of dedication. When we're dedicated to something or someone, we invest ourselves passionately—and before we know it, we get the feeling we're not appreciated to the measure of our contribution.

In certain kinds of situations and relationships, success is also an issue. It's hard to be humble when we see how good we are. And of course when we lose our humility we're open to all kinds of self-deception. We forget the people who taught us, the ones who have invested time and money and faith in us, and the God who has empowered us with talent. For a moment—and indeed, for longer—we think the whole world revolves around us. Elijah thought the future of Israel (and thus, the future of God's work in the world) rested upon him. Most of us have smaller worlds, so we come up with smaller complaints: our church, our school board, our team, our club, our family, our spouse's career—where would they be without me?

And as I indicated a bit earlier, weariness and fatigue often play a part. When we give ourselves earnestly to any cause or person, we can use up more energy than we can easily replace, and before long we're bone-weary, tired to the point of poor judgment, at which point self-pity comes in like a flood. And self-pity is the sorriest sibling of self-importance.

When we take ourselves too seriously, we're open to all kinds of serious errors. Kathleen Norris reminds us of a key insight from Michael O'Carroll: "Many heretics would have been saved if they had had a sense of humor."[1] My heresies are smaller, but no less ugly. I think of some of those times (fortunately, I can't remember them all) when I have been self-defensive. I would have done so well simply to have admitted that I was wrong, or have acknowledged the degree to which I was complicit in a given problem instead of proceeding as if I were above any failure. Ironically, very rarely is anything gained by proving someone else is in error. And by contrast, so much is sometimes gained when I can confess my fault, my part in a problem, because when I make such a confession, I can do something about the problem.

The world won't collapse if you or I admit that we are wrong. Even our own special world will survive—indeed, will almost surely improve. But it is difficult to admit when we are wrong if we take ourselves too seriously, because when we take ourselves too seriously, we dare not be wrong.

Well, let me tell you what happened to Elijah. God advised him of a fact Elijah didn't know: that there were seven thousand in Israel who hadn't bowed to Baal. Elijah thought he was the only one left on God's team, and God advised him that there was a deep bench. There probably wasn't another Elijah on the bench—a given generation can handle only so many Elijahs. But there were seven thousand out there who were ready to take their place when called upon.

I interrupt this report to note what God might properly have said: "Elijah, where and what were you before I elevated you to your present post, before I made you a personal (though unwelcome) advisor to the king, and a public personality? What was your public image? You were an unknown fellow in a poor suit, out there in Tishbe. Your name was unknown until I gave you this special assignment." As far as we know, God graciously omitted any such justified putdown with Elijah.

Because in truth Elijah was a very valuable property, as they might say on the sports page. He had performed magnificently, at a crucial time. But he wasn't indispensable, and he needed to know it. It's when we begin to see ourselves as indispensable that life gets all out of proportion and we take ourselves with embarrassing seriousness.

So God gave Elijah an interesting assignment. God sent him out to anoint two future kings and a prophetic successor to himself, the young farmer, Elisha. As it turns out, Elijah's anointing of Elisha is a peculiarly truncated affair. Elijah throws his mantle over Elisha, and recognizing the meaning of the act, Elisha asks for permission to bid his parents farewell before he follows Elijah. "Go back again," Elijah answers, "for what have I done to you?" (1 Kings 19:20). We're left to judge whether Elijah is withdrawing his offer, or is somewhat indifferent to Elisha, or whether Elijah is simply a brusque sort—something we had figured already. In any event, Elisha followed him—and in time, performed twice the miracles Elijah accumulated in his ministry, although still remaining in the shadow of Israel's most dramatic prophet.

You and I have our gifts from God and our place in the eternal enterprise. We play out our roles in different places and to different drummers. At times we're important, sometimes more than we begin to know—just as at other times we're not half as important as we're inclined to think. The secret is to know that we have a calling from God, and if it is from God, its size or its headline quality matters not at all. We can be secure enough to receive and benefit from candid self-evaluation, and wise enough to know that we're not indispensable. We're important. But not important enough to take ourselves so seriously.

That wise journalist, novelist, theologian, and devout believer, G. K. Chesterton, said, "Angels can fly because they take themselves lightly." Perhaps if you and I learn to take ourselves more lightly, we'll fly a bit, too.

NOTE

1. Kathleen Norris, *Amazing Grace* (New York: Riverhead Books, 1998), 357.

CHAPTER 4

Invest in Good Memories

When William J. Hyde, a pioneer preacher in the Midwest, was nearly ninety years old, a young minister asked him what he would preach about if he had only one sermon to preach.

Hyde answered that at that point in his life, it was an easy question to answer. The sermon would be on memories, and he'd like to preach it to a group of young people in their middle and late teens. "I would like to tell them that there are two things in life no person can get away from—himself and his memories." Hyde went on to explain that we can run away from home, school, community, responsibilities—almost everything except ourselves and our memories. "A store of good memories is the finest treasure a man can lay up on earth, while bad memories make hell out of this present life. 'Live so that your memories are good companions to the end of your days.' "[1]

Every year I live I realize more deeply the truth in William Hyde's words. My good memories are like a massive store of favorite movies that I can run across the screen of my mind while I walk or drive or sit in a tedious meeting. Some of these memories come unbidden and others I bring up at will, to make a pleasant interlude in time. By contrast the bad memories can intrude at even unlikely moments, sometimes on the sunniest of days; and I'm sure that some of those weird and bewildering dreams that come while we sleep have their genesis somewhere in a memory we would eliminate if we could. But the memories are there, so interwoven with our deepest person that only severing the soul from the spirit could take them from us—or the losing of the whole precious gift of memory.

This brings up a question that argues with the title of this chapter. We don't have to live long before we've invested in some bad memories. And while it's well enough to speak of investing in good ones, we also have some memories in which we didn't invest; others gave them to us, want them or not. Even the most fortunate of us—those who grow up in a loving home, with a covey of good friends and a measure of success in the classroom—can still recall some person who rejected us, some cutting word, some devastating experience. I want us to visit later about what to do with such memories, but for now let me acknowledge that not all our memories are of our own choosing. And with that, let me move into the general theme of memories.

I can't think of many subjects that are more biblically founded than this subject of memories. The Bible itself is an invitation to remember; indeed, by its existence it is essentially a command to do so. The prophets, apostles, and inspired historians who through the Holy Spirit left us with this Book did so because they believed there were some things we absolutely must remember and by recording their message they were making sure we would do so.

But more than that. The people of God in both the Hebrew Scriptures and in the New Testament established places and events that would help the memory process. As the children of Israel—not yet a nation, just a huge family of slaves—prepared to leave Egypt, their leader Moses said, "Remember this day on which you came out of Egypt, out of the house of slavery, because the LORD brought you out from there by strength of hand" (Exodus 13:3). *Remember!* The day of their deliverance was to be carved into their very souls, and they were given a day and a ritual to assist memory. And so it is that to this very day the descendants of Israel celebrate the event annually, in the Passover ceremonies.

This was only the first of a series of biblical holy days—days of celebration and of awe, but above all days of memory—that were written into the lives and psyches of Israel. We remember better if we have places on our calendars to assist our memory. This is why we need birthdays and anniversaries, not just because they provide an occasion for festivity but because they help us remember.

We have monuments for the same reason. When the generation after Moses crossed the Jordan River to establish a new home, they took twelve stones—a memory device in its own right, since the stones stood for the twelve sons of Israel—and built a makeshift monument, crude and simple, but a reminder that God had been with them in crossing the Jordan. A few generations later the nation's next truly great spiritual leader, Samuel, "took a stone and set it up between Mizpah and Jeshanah, and named it Ebenezer; for he said, 'Thus far the LORD has helped us'" (1 Samuel 7:12). The stone was to remind the nation that the Lord had brought them thus far and that they therefore could be assured that the future, too, was in God's strong hand.

And we, too, have our monuments. Sometimes they belong to the community, commemorating figures from our local or national history, and sometimes they are the private cemetery markers for family members. And in America as in many countries we've gone farther to make sure the monuments themselves are not forgotten, by having a Memorial Day. Most of us have some other "monuments," souvenirs of days gone by—mementoes of a relationship, of a vacation, of one of life's special persons or occasions.

Remember. On the night before our Lord's crucifixion he met to eat with his disciples and during the meal added a special element. Taking bread and wine, he told the little group to see these elements as his body and blood and, "Do this, as often as you drink it, in remembrance of me"

(1 Corinthians 11:25). So it is that believers around the world—some occasionally, some weekly, some daily—have a ritual of memory.

An important element in these ceremonies of memory—whether calendar events or physical monuments—is to guide our memories in productive paths. You and I gather plenty of memories, pick them up every day at one level of quality or another; gather them willy nilly, without effort and sometimes against our will. But the Scriptures teach us to be wise in collecting right memories, memories that will enhance our lives and give them unique beauty and substance. Memories are far too powerful to be left to chance; we should guide the process to productive ends. It's clear enough that some useless and destructive memories will find a place in our minds and souls regardless, so we'd better work at using our gift of memory to holy profit.

One secret is to seek out special occasions. Some come to us custom-made, like Independence Day, Thanksgiving, and Christmas. But even such conventional memory-makers need to be cultured, because if not treated carefully they can become commonplace; and if mishandled they sometimes develop bad memories rather than good ones. Don't be afraid to invest love in such special days—and if your effort doesn't get the desired result, don't give up. We're dealing with humans, you know, folks made of the same sometimes-insensitive stuff as ourselves. Work for beauty in memories even if sometimes others seem negligent or even obstructive. When you have good traditions, add to them but don't be afraid to let new ones come to birth.

Food is a remarkable nurturer of memories. It isn't by chance that the great religious occasions of the Old Testament were feast days—or that the primary celebration of the Christian faith is a "meal," Holy Communion. Something about eating together opens the soul to memories. The poet Conrad Aiken was recalling a particular individual when he wrote, "And bread I broke with you was more than bread," but all who read the poem bring up persons and scenes of their own. I remember fried potatoes, Wonder bread, and radishes on summer evenings in my boyhood: not very healthy fare, I fear, but I see my mother and father at the table as I recall that menu.

I remember my first malted milk. I was working for two weeks, at a dollar a day, as hopper on a laundry delivery truck, and the driver asked me if I'd like to stop for a malted milk. I was ashamed to ask what it was, so I just said, "Sure!"—and was thereby introduced to one of life's simple, lovely luxuries. I remember the evening when Rae Wetmore took our boys' Sunday school class to see her place of business, then to a restaurant for dinner (we called it supper), a grand experience for teenagers from the Helping Hand Mission. And at a very different level, I remember dinner at a café in Paris when my daughter was teaching there for a year. And lunches with friends in the Rotary club, and potluck suppers in so many churches that I wonder how it is that numbers of them have singular places in my memory. Janet and I eat out occasionally, but we favor dinner for two in our own home, followed by prayer. I choose often to have lunch with my students, or with colleagues, and with my son on study retreats—times for vigorous conversation and rolling laughter. What better place for memories to come to birth than at a meal—breakfast, lunch, dinner, supper, picnic, coffee shop—you name the place, and a memory will come across the screen of your soul.

Faith occasions give us memories, and our memories keep those faith occasions alive. A freshman girl from Wisconsin and a graduate student from the South began sitting in the same pew at the First United Methodist Church in Madison, Wisconsin. Several years later I was privileged to perform their wedding, and a few weeks later they asked me to dedicate their first home in a trailer park. I remember the occasion well: Ann and Jerry and Ann's parents and I crowded into very limited quarters to read scripture and a liturgy of dedication. Some twenty years later, I was in their home again—this time a beautiful lakefront property in

Indiana, where Jerry was a vice president of an international manufacturer, and their teenage daughters were at the table. When we joined hands for the table grace, I thought of that trailer park in Madison, Wisconsin, and I thanked God for holy memories—and that Ann and Jerry had chosen to begin their home with just such memories.

Our memories play tricks on us, of course—sometimes to good and sometimes to ill. In his biography of Geoffrey Studdert Kennedy, William Purcell says that the French remembered the summer of 1914, just before World War I broke out, as a time of "exceptional splendor; the trees never so heavy, the fields never so rich"; and that years later, "the British were to feel exactly the same about the summer of 1940"—and that we tend to do the same with personal memories, giving them color that exists "only in the eye of recollection."[2] Just as surely, we sometimes cast a heavy pall on some life chapters by the way we set some person or event into our memory's store.

But what about the memories we wish were never there, the kind that would make a Shakespearean character cry, "Out, damned spot, out I say!"[3] The adjective is strong but well-chosen, because some memories seem to damn us, to take our very souls hostage. What can be done with such memories?

Take them first to a place where there's better perspective. I speak of the cross of Christ. At the cross we see life and its issues in the light of the ultimate. At the cross there is not only supreme sacrifice but also—at the first—utter defeat. But beyond the cross there is resurrection, a righting of all that is wrong. The cross puts the daily and monthly and annual stuff of life under the scope of eternity and that makes all the difference. At the cross we get a quite different perspective on not only our pain and defeat but also on our pleasures and accomplishments. And we know that all of life's accounts aren't settled in September. There is more to life than the hurt someone has given to me or the pain I've inflicted on another.

With this realization we get the freedom to deal with our problems—at least, with those that can still be dealt with. The larger tragedy in our bad memories is that they limit our ability to fight back and to go on. When our memories are put in perspective, we are freer to do whatever can still be done. Prayer is a special ally. Now and again I think of someone I have hurt but who is now many years removed from my life but still in a corner of my memory. I can still pray for these persons—carefully, specifically, and earnestly. I have no way of finding them, but I can pray for them; they aren't lost to God. In truth, I may serve them better by my prayers than by anything I did or might have done in person at some earlier time.

Time and faith also put the past and its memories into perspective. No story says this better than the biblical story of Joseph and his brothers. When Joseph was only seventeen and obnoxious to his older brothers for his precociousness and his father's favoritism, his brothers sold him into slavery. Half a generation later, Joseph was second in command in Egypt and in a position to destroy his brothers or at least to get revenge for their malice against him. The brothers were sure Joseph would get revenge. But Joseph had the perspective of years and of the unfolding of the providence of God. "Even though you intended to do harm to me," Joseph said, "God intended it for good" (Genesis 50:20).

Joseph got the long view, the view that comes by faith. In his case, he had the additional advantage of the unfolding of time and circumstances. Blessed are those who, even without such fortuitous events, are still able to leave matters in the hands of God and the working of time and eternity. I'm not suggesting that we wait for revenge; revenge is not our business and the thought of it corrupts the soul. I speak of seeing life on a larger stage, where we know there's more to life than the scoreboards our culture so easily establishes. There are things that sometimes must be worked out in courts of law and justice, but a pure heart is worth more than monetary satisfaction, and a tranquil spirit than a pound of flesh.

And we can help our memories by giving them something new to work with. I think so often of my late friend, Ed. I have seen few people so devastated by the loss of a spouse. He watched with her through months of suffering, then tried to rebuild his life after her death. But the memories were too great, memories of nearly fifty years of a remarkably happy marriage. He worked harder at his service activities in a community organization, involved himself more than ever with his church and his Sunday school class, but somehow all of these things only accentuated memories of Dorothy and the days when she had also been part of these groups and events.

Then, almost by chance and hardly with his full acquiescence, Ed joined a group of fellow church members for a trip to the British Isles. In the group he found new friends, and new excitement in old friends—and with it all, a daily flood of the stuff from which memories are made. The enforced camaraderie of a tour bus, the incidents that would be mildly amusing at home but that were strangely hilarious in another world, the daily banter of tour mates, and the end-of-the-day group devotions: all of these added up to a whole new world of memories.

The new memories in no way diminished Ed's memories of a beautiful marriage, but they gave him new memories on which to dwell. Instead of retreating so often to a cellar of lonely memories, he inhabited a new dining area of recent memories that now held promise for new days and memories still to come. Since you and I live in the house of memories that we have built—and that others have helped build for us—we need to keep adding new, beautiful rooms to that house. For as long as we live.

And we need to choose which rooms we will inhabit. Sometimes when I am very alone, driving my automobile or sitting in an airplane or falling asleep, unwelcome memories—and destructive ones—clamor for my attention. At such times, sometimes I pray, but sometimes also I look into my store of my private movies: those persons, places, and incidents from my past that make me smile. And I consciously choose to put my mind on those pleasant memories until the ugly ones are crowded out. By God's grace I can choose the places in my house of memories where I will dwell.

Meanwhile, I keep investing in still more good memories. You'll find me in memory's marketplace sometime today.

NOTES

1. William J. Hyde, *Dig or Die, Brother Hyde* (as told to Harriet Harmon Dexter) (New York: Harper and Bros., 1954), 232.

2. William Purcell, *Woodbine Willie* (London: Hodder & Stoughton, 1962), 74-75.

3. William Shakespeare, *Macbeth*, V, i, 38.

CHAPTER 5

Make Friends of Your Regrets

Before I go even a word farther, let me say that this rule of the good life—"Make friends of your regrets"—has its hazards. No doubt this is why some thoughtful people have given quite opposite counsel. Ludwig Boerne, the early nineteenth-century German author, disposed of regret with no exceptions: "To regret nothing is the beginning of all wisdom." Jerome K. Jerome, the English novelist and playwright from later in that century, probably had something of the same attitude in mind when he wrote, "Opportunities flit by while we sit regretting the chances we have lost." Most of us have known someone whose life was controlled by some regret or compilation of regrets from long years before. I think there are persons of whom it could be said that their obituaries could have been written the day they began regretting some grievous error or choice, because from that point on, the person ceased to live. All the years that followed were controlled by an overpowering regret.

I confess, too, that I am myself more than a little prone to regret. I know some of my regrets are quite foolish. When I come to a particular four-way stop in our city, I still remember an evening five or six years ago when I lost count of my turn and went ahead of another driver—an act which caused him anger; probably more than necessary but justified nevertheless. No harm was suffered except for the irritation the other, unknown driver felt (irritation that he expressed with his horn), but I regret it yet. Very silly of me. Other regrets are more substantive. I have wrestled with them, and have sought to make amends where possible. And with it all, I have concluded that regrets have a valid and productive place in the life of the spirit, and that if treated with care they can bless their owner. Treated unwisely, they come rather to own us, in which case regret is a subtle, quite relentless enemy.

In some ways, regret is like anger. Anger is a very powerful force; indeed, a necessary one. I submit that a substantial share of human progress has come about because of anger well-directed. If a group of nineteenth-century women had not become angry at the injustice of being without a vote, there would never have been a nineteenth amendment to the Constitution. It was the anger of a great many Americans, white and black—anger to the point of blood in the case of John Brown and Nat Turner—that eventually led to the end of slavery in the United States. Anger has fueled the engine of reform at every level of life—anger against poverty, against judicial injustice, against ignorance—and without that anger, much moral and economic and social progress would never have happened. But just as surely, uncontrolled anger has worked far-reaching tragedy.

And so it is with regret. Regret can be useless and self-defeating, as in those instances where people destroy much of their lives regretting a bad decision or an unfortunate choice. "For of all sad words of tongue or pen," wrote John Greenleaf Whittier, "The saddest are these: 'It might have been.'"[1] I don't know that anyone has ever put Whittier's words on a tombstone, but they could well be written on ten thousands of hearts, in lives that have forfeited living at a place of regretting.

Let me say without hesitancy that I wouldn't want to live in a world where no one had a capacity for regret. As a lieutenant colonel in the Nazi secret police, Adolf Eichmann played a key role in the killing of some six million Jews during World War II. But after his apprehension and while awaiting trial in Israel, he said, "To sum it all up, I must say I regret nothing." I can't imagine a world where people could think that way. I vote rather with G. Campbell Morgan, who was not only a great preacher but a person of sensitive conscience. "If any man can look back on the past years with complete satisfaction, he is a shallow, superficial sort of man."[2] The progress of the human race can be measured, I submit, in how as individuals and as nations we respond to those instances in the past when we have been guilty in our treatment of either our enemies or our friends. It isn't often possible to repent effectively for the sins of our ancestors, but we can acknowledge them and make sure that we do not repeat them.

There is a place in life, an important place, for community regret—the sorrow we feel for what our generation, or humanity, has done. We may or may not be complicit, but we know we must remember so that perhaps we can prevent history from repeating itself. A Lexington, Kentucky, physician of my acquaintance, Lt. Col. Ralph D. Caldroney, reported recently on some of his experiences as a medical officer in the United States Army in Afghanistan. After describing a poignant moment of official farewell as a coffin was loaded on a transport plane, he asked, "Will this memory stay with me?" He gave answer in the next sentence: "I hope so. For if I can't recall and maintain these ever-so-poignant times, then I will have lost some of my soul and much of my humanity."[3]

As for our own, personal misconduct—in deeds or in words—regret is the beginning of renewal and change. Healthy regret begins when we have the grace and intelligence to examine our conduct objectively against an honorable standard. I've found that I do well to ask myself how I would feel if the roles were reversed. When I see myself as the object of a deed rather than as its initiator, my feelings can be materially different. Sometimes this is ineffective, however, because our culture or lifestyle may be quite different from that of the person who feels injured. In such instances we need to imagine how we would feel if we had that person's background. To put it in simple geographic terms: how would I respond to a particular act if I were a native of the Far East, with deeply ingrained culture patterns from that heritage. What I've done might not offend me as an occidental, but it would be very different if I had an Asian heritage.

Regret should then lead to amends. Be very grateful if your experience of regret comes at a time when amends are still possible. In my years as a pastor I led many funeral services where some friend or family member sat with pain that seemed beyond healing, because they knew they could have made things "right" if they had acted in time, but now that time was past. Death had taken the opportunity for direct amends. But be prepared for the kind of person or circumstance where your amends are not accepted. For some people the grievance is too deep for healing, at least at the moment of your offer. And there are persons, of course, who prefer the stagnant waters of resentment over forgiveness and healing. If your attempt at healing has been rejected and if upon further examination you are satisfied that your attempt was faithfully offered, be done with the matter until a more opportune time. If such a time never comes, be at peace with the knowledge that you've done what you could.

What about those regrets where the greatest harm has been to our own souls? What we've done may have had a wide peripheral fallout, but the largest sorrow has been our own; what then? Let regret have its perfect work. See it as an opportunity for inner cleansing and for spiritual growth. I think of Oscar Wilde's poignant words: "How else but through a broken heart / May Lord Christ enter in?"[4] I can't think of many writers with a greater gift for easy cynicism, but all of that quality is gone in this poem written during Wilde's incarceration. But his Catholic heritage asserted itself. He recognized that his brokenness—the pain of regret—was the best of all entries for the Lord Christ. Our Lord accepts whatever throne we may offer, but no offer is more sincere and more substantial than that which comes through grief, as expressed in a broken heart.

This kind of regret opens the possibility of a birth of new character. Professor Alan Jacobs reminds us of St. Augustine's insight on human memory, which I think is effectively related to the experience of wholesome regret. Such memory, Augustine taught, "is not mere recollection. Memory allows one not only to recall but also to reconstruct, to reinterpret past events, to discern a pattern in them that was not visible when they occurred."[5] It is by our regrets that we grow. Regrets generally represent the refuse of our lives, the stuff we'd like simply to eliminate from memory—both ours and that of our community of friends and associates. But these regrets can become the compost of the soul, the place where new life grows best.

This is the first great benefit in making friends of our regrets. Having found peace with God in true repentance, regret provides a setting for quality growth in character. This growth will probably begin with honest humility. For instance, regret puts our accomplishments in proportion. Where previously we may have thought of ourselves as rather remarkable, when we face up to the errors we have made or the sins we've committed, we get a better plumb line by which to measure the integrity of our achievements. This won't diminish any real achievement or any accomplishment of real substance. But it will clear out the superficial and will leave us with those elements of our work and character which are of worth.

Intelligent regret also makes us more sympathetic and understanding of the faults and failures of others. A man in a search committee said that he would never hire an inexperienced person for any job. I wondered where that man got his first position! I was sorry that he had forgotten his early failures, that there wasn't enough regret in his psyche to make him sympathetic with those who are relatively untried. I would hate to work for an employer with a poor memory—that is, for someone who had no regrets. And come to think of it, I'd hate to sit in a congregation where the preacher had no regrets. Men and women write better sermons when regrets check them from paragraph to paragraph with questions: Remember that time you stumbled? Remember the word you spoke when you should have swallowed it? A good sense of regret wonderfully improves the way we look upon other people in their time of need or failure or shame.

Healthy regrets can drive us on to better accomplishments. I think of a missionary priest in an otherwise-forgotten novel. People wondered at his indefatigable energy and his untiring readiness to serve—except for those few who knew of an earlier sexual indiscretion and the regret the priest was still striving to pay back. I think often of a friend from half a century ago who labored for Christ with seemingly endless vigor. When people asked his secret, his answer was always the same: "From eighteen to twenty-seven, I used all my energy for the devil. I intend to spend the rest of my life using my energy for Christ."

Regret helps us avoid repeating our mistakes, our sins, our natural stupidities. This makes the future a more secure investment. A man attending a convention dropped out of a group as they set out for an evening of decidedly marginal entertainment. "I've traveled that road already," he said, with more apology than superiority. "I don't want to go there again."

Regret is the redeeming residue of guilt. Guilt that is not taken to a place of divine forgiveness and beginning-again will only destroy. But guilt that has been forgiven can then lead us to a wholesome level of regret. People who wallow in guilt reject both the fullness of salvation and the mercy of God. But people who treat guilt casually put themselves in peril of repeating their error. A good dose of true regret can prevent such serial behavior.

One of my personal regrets has to do with the poor way

I've sometimes handled my regrets. I would have done better at several places in my life if I had acted on my regrets sooner. That is, it would have been so much better if I had sought sooner to make right as much as possible of what was wrong. I don't think there is any perfect time for making amends—except of course to do so while it is still possible. Beyond that, it's hard to say, because while the time may be right for the perpetrator, it may not be so for the victim—and in all such matters, the victim is the one deserving consideration. Then, beyond that, I wish I had sometimes worked more intentionally toward change. I wish I had been a better student of my own soul and had seen not only my failure but also what I might do by way of remedy and improvement. In the words of that perceptive nineteenth-century British novelist George Eliot, "The terror of being judged sharpens the memory....Intense memory forces a man to own his blameworthy past."[6] One needs to *own* his or her past—not wallow in it, nor revel in it, but admit that it belongs to him or her—and then to let the past be a qualified instructor.

But as I warned earlier, regret has its perils. Indeed, I know of no virtue, no opportunity in life, no talent that is not accompanied by a companion danger, and regret is no exception to that rule. There's no question but that regret can destroy. There have been times in Christian history when regret has become a kind of religious industry, organized and practiced according to some generally recognized rules. *Flagellation* was the key idea—and more particularly, self-flagellation: beating one's self because for some reason one has the feeling that such suffering is deserved—and if no one else has recognized the need and administered the suffering, the person should inflict it upon himself. There was a medieval European sect that administered such scourging in public.

I submit that for every medieval physical flagellant there are currently ten thousand or more emotional flagellants in our day—earnest, sensitive people who lacerate their souls with pointless regrets. While proper regret leads to gracious and more productive living, unhealthy regret makes for a kind of interior suicide, a self-loathing that hurts its victim and a good many innocent bystanders.

In the hours following Jesus' crucifixion two men notably experienced regret. Peter, who denied his Lord three times, even to the point of blasphemy, "broke down and wept" in his bitter regret (Mark 14:72)—but returned to Christ and eventually to magnificent service until his own martyrdom. Judas, too, felt regret, felt it so deeply that he threw down the money he had been paid for betraying Jesus. But he wouldn't let go of his regret, and "he went and hanged himself" (Matthew 27:5). I believe Judas's regret was as sincere as Peter's, but for him regret became an end in itself, rather than a step toward healing and a new life.

David Paul Deavel urges that we live in such fashion that we have "as little moral regret in life as possible." Listen to God's warnings, he recommends, rather than waiting until we need forgiveness. But all of us, even the greatest souls, have reasons for regret, and the secret then is to use regret rather than becoming its prisoners. As Deavel goes on to say, it is only when we regret our sins that we come "to realize how merciful God is and how much it is that we owe to God. Given that fact, whether we are 18 or 80, we should want a few regrets."[7]

I've known regret in a variety of forms over the years of my life, and I'm afraid that I've honored it with many hours of servitude. I've learned that if I don't use regret, it will abuse me. That is, I've learned that it's up to me as to whether regret is my ally or my enemy. I've decided it's better by far to make friends of my regrets—but all the while choosing that friendship with great care.

NOTES

1. John Greenleaf Whittier, *Maud Muller*, st. 53.

2. G. Campbell Morgan, *In the Shadow of Grace* (Grand Rapids: Baker Books, 2007), 118.

3. Ralph D. Caldroney, "Holding onto humanity by connecting to war's loss," *Lexington Herald Leader*, 5-31-2010, A-11.

4. Oscar Wilde, *The Ballad of Reading Gaol*.

5. Alan Jacobs, *Looking Before and After* (Grand Rapids, Mich.: William B. Eerdmans, 2008), 42.

6. George Eliot, *Middlemarch*, Volume 8, 197.

7. David Paul Deavel, "Regretfully yours," *Christian Century*, Volume 126, No.18 (September 8, 2009), 36.

CHAPTER 6

Be Glad God Knows You So Well

I am grateful for friendship at any level, but especially for friendships that have both length and depth. I had such a friendship with Bill. We knew each other briefly in the fifth grade, then became lifelong friends in high school with a friendship that is still with me in many ways, although Bill died nearly five years ago.

It was a friendship where we invested the time and the emotional and spiritual energy necessary to know each other well. Friendships of this quality have a high price, which is one reason we don't get many of them. But of course there's an indefinable quality in great friendships which has nothing to do with logic or even with our willingness to sacrifice for one another. It's hard to explain why some people become our lifelong friends while others, with what seems to be a more fitting personality profile, never become more than Christmas greeting friends. Whatever it is that makes for a great friendship, there has to be this mutual willingness for the friendship to go below the surface, down to the roots of personality and caring.

It helped that Bill always thought well of me. He didn't always agree with me; in fact, we often had vigorous discussions that even became arguments. Nor did he always approve of my choices, nor did I of his conduct. But once a course of action was taken, we supported one another one hundred percent. Bill was very intelligent and also very intuitive, so I often took more comfort in his opinions than I should have, assuming that his approval demonstrated that I really was a better-than-average sort of person. It's nice to have at least one person like that in your life, someone who knows you well but still thinks well of you, so you'll forgive me for prizing his opinion too highly.

But of course Bill was fallible, and he also had to die. That's why I have a predicament from time to time when I come to a desert place where I'd like to express some less-than-noble opinions without being thought less-than-noble. I say to myself, "I wish Bill was still here. I'd like to talk with him about this." It's important to have a friend who knows you well and who still likes you.

Herein is one of the loveliest facts I know about God. God knows everything about me, including some occasional thoughts that I hate to acknowledge even to myself as being part of who I am, and yet God keeps on loving me. God has divinely impeccable taste, and finds me attractive! How remarkable! How reassuring! How full of hope for my continuing welfare! And how good to know at those times when some people with less-than-divine taste voice other judgments regarding me.

Mind you, God thinks I could stand some improvement, and makes this very clear to me when I'm willing to listen. But God thinks that with divine help I'm capable of whatever improvement is needed, and this makes all the difference. Heaven's judgment on my soul never disheartens me, because I know the judgment is fair and I know it is delivered in love, and I know that even when the judgment identifies my shortcomings it comes with the confidence that by God's grace I can make it.

I suppose it is these elements that make Psalm 139 one of my favorite chapters in the Bible—indeed, in all of literature of any kind. It is a psalm attributed to King David, a person with a passion for friendship, as demonstrated by his legendary ties with Jonathan and by the kind of loyalty he evoked from his soldiers and his political and religious associates. David knew something about human friendship, and cherished it. But most of all, he marveled at the privilege of friendship with God.

"O LORD, you have searched me and known me," David wrote. How well? "You know when I sit down and when I rise up." Yes, and more than that: "You discern my thoughts from far away" (Psalm 139:1-2).

There's a clear implication in this language. If someone cares about something as inconsequential as my sitting down and my getting up (the ultimate Twitter-friend!), I must be very important to that person. And if I have even a modicum of modesty, I want to say to that person, "Don't you have anything better to do with your time?" If you had suggested to David that God must have better things to do than to keep such a record of his physical activity, David might have answered, "This isn't a measure of my importance but of God's generosity. God chooses to see such value in me that even my ordinary pursuits have extraordinary worth in his sight."

So, too, with our thoughts. Why would God want to know the psalmist's thoughts "from far away"? Folks used to say, when a friend seemed unduly quiet, "A penny for your thoughts"; and sometimes the friend would reply, "My thoughts aren't worth much more than that"—and as I recall, even at that cost they were sometimes overpriced. If one has a friend like Samuel Johnson, who is likely at any moment to drop a phrase that ought to be recorded, it would be worthwhile to know their thoughts "from far away." But most of our thoughts are pretty mundane, not always coherent, and sometimes better forgotten. Yet the psalmist was sure that God cared for him so much that even his random ramblings had worth. So much worth, in fact, that God was interested while those thoughts were still in the process of unfolding, still in the um-ah-well-yeah state. As you read on in Psalm 139, you realize that the writer doesn't always find pleasure in this divine attention. At times, in fact, he has tried to flee from it. But then he realizes how useless such a flight is. God has known him, after all, since he was in his mother's womb: "When I was being made in secret... / Your eyes beheld my unformed substance" (139:15-16).

So we should remember that if we get involved in a friendship with God, we'll discover that God is paying more attention to us than we necessarily want. Why is it then that we have in our souls a longing for God's friendship? And why is it, that want it or not, we need this friendship?

The book of Genesis, with its profound wisdom, tells us the secret. It explains our need of human relationship in the story of Adam and Eve: with all the wonders of the creation about him, including the wonderful animal kingdom, still "there was not found a helper as his partner," so God "took one of his ribs," and that rib God "made into a woman" (Genesis 2:20-22). God had said, "It is not good that the man should be alone" (Genesis 2:18). We human creatures are by our very nature communicating creatures, and we need others with whom to communicate. Even for the most introverted of us, it's isn't quite enough to talk with ourselves. So we need friends.

But prior to this story, Genesis tells another fact about us: that when God created us, we were taken from the very "dust of the ground," but that God "breathed into [our] nostrils the breath of life" (Genesis 2:7). The breath that is in us is divine breath. There is something of God in us, no matter how badly we treat ourselves, and that breath of God within us insists on communication with the reality of the God who in-breathed us at our creation. So we need the divine friendship. We are poor—destitute!—unless we have some communion with God. We creatures of dust, who walk on the dust and will return to it, are at the same time creatures of eternity, with God's breath in us, the breath always clamoring for its proper place in our lives.

So I need this friendship, and so do you. I can ignore it,

resent it, flee from it, curse it. But I can't fully live without it. And no matter how intellectually, socially, and culturally alert I am without God, I can't estimate how much more I will become if God is in my life—and not only in my life, but in it to the degree that he desires. So, too, no matter how many friends bless my life on this earth and no matter how I cherish and nurture those friendships, there is part of me that no human friendship can fill. You and I are made for friendship with God. I referred earlier to the fine writer, Katherine Mansfield, who couldn't believe in a personal God yet yearned to be able to give thanks to someone beyond herself. She expressed the same hunger for such a divine friendship. "It seems to me there is a great change come over the world since people like us believed in God," she wrote to a friend. "Yet we must believe; and not only that—we must carry our weakness and our sin and our devilishness to somebody . . .we must feel that we are *known* (italics hers), that our hearts are known, as God knew us."[1] We need a Friend who knows us *well*.

Human friends, even the best and saintliest of them, have their limitations. We have no right to expect any human being to put up with us all the time. Our friends have lives of their own and problems and joys of their own and to expect them to push aside matters that are dear to them or demanding of them in order always to pay attention to us is the ultimate self-centeredness. Self-centered people rarely realize this, however, because since they occupy the center of life as they know it, they find everyone else just slightly peripheral.

And of course other humans can never get all the way into our souls, nor should they. When we love someone deeply, whether as friends or romantically, we often expect them to understand everything about us. Again, this is too much to ask. And in truth, sometimes we discover we don't like it if people understand us too well. We want them to understand enough to sympathize and empathize but not to criticize or reform. Our friendship with God sometimes upsets us at just this point. We want God to understand us enough to sympathize with our pain and perhaps to heal it, but not to reveal our pettiness and sin. Thus we are likely to back off from God at just the point when our relationship might be most beneficial.

Can I let God into my life all the way? Ultimately only God can answer that question, because only God knows how complex and many-parted you and I are. Some of us who have bowed at altars of dedication have promised God that we are now entirely his, but the more honest of us have realized a few hours or days or weeks later that this is only theoretically so. One problem is that you and I—even the dullest of us—are constantly changing and growing, so the person who dedicates wholly to God on Wednesday needs to do so again by Friday or Saturday, because he or she has changed in the meanwhile. God can keep up with this, but it's harder for us to realize our changing need and to welcome God's continued inward renewing.

But because there is no friendship remotely to be compared with our potential friendship with God, we should seek constantly to keep it up-to-date, and to seek God's presence in even the least auspicious and least attractive places in our lives. And we should be ready for the fact that God understands us better than we sometimes want to be understood. I remember times in my life as a pastor-counselor when someone complained, "No one understands me," when in truth they were understood very well—and didn't like it! God understands me. He knows "my downsitting and my uprising," and while at times this makes me uncomfortable, I need badly to be so completely understood. I cherish the possibility that because God understands me I may come to a better understanding of myself—and that as a result, I will make some improvements on myself.

Our friendship with God helps balance and correct our other friendships. Sometimes other persons underestimate us: I have known people who were never rightly appreciated by friends or family, and in such instances I've prayed that God would assure them of their inestimable worth. On the other hand, we may receive superficial praise that needs the correcting that comes from an eternal vantage point. God's friendship provides the wholesome balance we need.

A growing friendship with God makes us better suited for our human friendships. I say this cautiously because I know well enough that religion is sometimes misused, and that some people use faith issues to distance and alienate themselves from others. But over the decades I have found that the greatest souls and the people most capable of loyal friendship are those who have a deep friendship with God. But again, a qualifying word: deep faith doesn't necessarily make people of very different personalities good friends. Other, quite unreligious matters also contribute to the stuff that makes up friendship. No matter: as we draw closer to God and accept God's correction and refinement of our hearts and minds, we are better able to participate in meaningful human relationships.

But let me return to where I began. The quality that makes for truly great human friendships has both length and depth. It proves itself over time, and it goes deep into the parties involved. The same is true, magnified immeasurably, in our friendship with God. I am quite sure that the loneliness we humans sometimes feel—the quiet ache that comes even when we are with the persons who mean most to us, as well as in times of separation—is loneliness for the eternal nearness of God. Something in our souls wants to feel that the breath we are about to take has in it something of God's breath. We know, and we cannot deny, that there is more to us than a bone and a hank of hair. We are from God, and when day's work is done—or indeed, sometimes when it is most upon us—we want to feel that God is there: our Friend.

Charles Wesley, the co-founder of the Methodist movement of the eighteenth century and the author of some seven thousand hymns, has a great phrase in one of these hymns: *"My name is written on His hands."* [2] It is one of the most jubilant of Wesley hymns—and he specialized in songs of gladness!—but it seems clear that the hymn was written after a time of deep, inward turmoil. It begins, "Arise, my soul, arise; / Shake off thy guilty fears." That is, Wesley was struggling—as any sensitive soul will from time to time—with the fears that come from guilt and a sense of failure. But facing those "guilty fears" directly, Wesley reassures himself that he can never be forgotten by his Lord; his name is written on the very hands of Christ.

I sense that Wesley is making two allusions in that powerful phrase. He is no doubt reflecting on the words of the prophet Isaiah, when the prophet was reassuring his people that they were not forgotten by God. "Can a woman forget her nursing child?" God asks rhetorically through the prophet, then continues, "See, I have inscribed you on the palms of my hands" (Isaiah 49:15-16). At the same time, Charles Wesley is thinking of our Lord's death at Calvary ("Five bleeding wounds he bears," Wesley writes later in the hymn) and takes strength in the confidence that the wounds in the hands of Christ bear his name: such is the significance of Christ's death for our salvation.

And such is the continuing assurance of the place we have by way of our divine friendship. We have this indelible, ineffaceable place in God's thinking. The Bible's salvation story teaches us that our value before God is so great that God's Son has died for our salvation—and more yet, that the Holy Spirit pursues us, seeking to reconcile us to God.

And this is why I am glad that God knows me so well—and why, for your sake, I'm glad God knows you, too. As I said at the outset, I was blessed in a human friendship by a lifelong friend who knew me well, yet continued to think kindly of me. But as much as I cherished Bill's friendship, it pales beside the friendship I have known in God. This One who knows when I sit down and when I arise, who knows my thoughts before I can quite shape them on my tongue:

this God thinks kindly of me. It is not a divine sentimentality, because God doesn't like everything I do, or say, or think. Sometimes I offend him dreadfully in the ways I fall short of his best expectations.

But God loves me enough to see my continuing potential, and to prod me on when I get weary of myself. As the days and weeks of life go by, I want increasingly for God to find more pleasure in me. I owe God that much, for knowing me so well and still desiring my friendship.

NOTES

1. Henry Sloane Coffin, *Joy in Believing* (New York: Charles Scribner's Sons, 1956), 13.

2. Charles Wesley, "Arise, My Soul, Arise," *The Methodist Hymnal* (Nashville: The Methodist Publishing House, 1964, 1966), 122.

CHAPTER 7

Fall in Love with Your Rainy Days

I'm glad I'm old enough to have seen the movie musical in which Gene Kelly dances rapturously in the midst of a drenching downpour, all the while singing "I'm Singin' in the Rain." The male lead in the movie, played by Kelly, has just fallen in love and nothing about the weather or the traffic or the people who wonder if he's lost his senses can interfere with his happiness.

When Betty Comden and Adolph Green, the writers, showed the scene to Leonard Bernstein, Bernstein said, "That scene is an affirmation of life."[1] Obviously I don't know all that was in Mr. Bernstein's mind when he spoke as he did, but I understand enough that I want to say, "My thoughts exactly!" The weather was against dancing and singing. It was, in fact, weather for staying indoors, feet on an ottoman, near a blazing fireplace. But the hero in the movie knows better. He is celebrating life, and his celebration can't be shut down by something as incidental as a drenching downpour.

Every life has its share of the inclement. I've known some people who have seemed to me to have more than their share of such weather. But as I've observed us humans for a series of decades, I've discovered that it isn't the weather—or to put it another way, the particular fortunes and misfortunes of life—that determine how people feel. It is the attitude we bring to our circumstances. The people who live victoriously are those who learn to fall in love with their rainy days.

When we refer to the apostle Paul as Saint Paul we're generally thinking of his role in bringing the gospel to Europe and his major contribution to Christian belief via his letters. But I have a more pragmatic view: I like the way Paul handled his rainy days. And he had plenty of them. It was in such days that he earned his saintly credentials.

If I read Paul's personality rightly, he wasn't the sort of person who was easily satisfied. Let's just say that he had quite sophisticated tastes. His father held Roman citizenship, which was automatically passed on to Paul. He studied under one of the great scholars of his time. When he was still young, he decided to pursue membership in the Pharisees, the most elite and demanding of the Jewish religious orders.

But when he chose to follow Jesus Christ, he lost virtually all of his former advantages. Still worse, he made himself vulnerable to frequent arrest and public trial—and at times to the humiliation of stonings and floggings. But worst of all, as I understand Paul's temperament, he was forced at times to depend on charity, on the goodwill of others. He loved to boast that he paid his own way. Other apostles were supported by the gifts of believers, but Paul worked as a tentmaker, so he could support himself and be independent of the congregations to whom he preached.

But incarcerated in Rome, unable to follow his tent-making trade, Paul wrote to thank the church at Philippi for their support. He was grateful, truly grateful, but still he made light of his need: "For I have learned to be content with whatever I have. I know what it is to have little, and I know what it is to have plenty. In any and all circumstances I have learned the secret of being well-fed and of going hungry, of having plenty and of being in need. I can do all things through him who strengthens me" (Philippians

4:11-13). Paul had grown up as a child of privilege and was very comfortable in such a world. But he came to fall in love with his rainy days. Mind you, it wasn't a matter of gritting his teeth and making the best of it—because in truth, we really don't make the best of it by gritting our teeth but by opening our mouth in a grand smile or in giving forth with a belly laugh. Paul learned the wonder of being in love with where he was.

Frederick Buechner, that remarkable novelist and theologian, tells of such a time when he was serving with the Army. His battalion was on bivouac somewhere near Anniston, Alabama. The sun had gone down, and a cold drizzle was adding to the mud and general misery. He was still hungry, and when he saw that a soldier nearby had a turnip left over, he asked if he might have it. The man tossed it to him, but Buechner missed the catch and the turnip fell in the mud. Buechner picked it up and ate it anyway, mud and all. Buechner writes that he saw suddenly that not only was the turnip good, but the mud and drizzle and cold were good, and even the Army he had so long dreaded. He continues, "Sitting there in the Alabama winter with my mouth full of cold turnip and mud, I could see at least for a moment how if you ever took truly to heart the ultimate goodness and joy of things, even at their bleakest, the need to praise someone or something for it would be so great that you might even have to go out and speak of it to the birds of the air."[2]

There's a wonderful toughness in this attitude toward life. When Paul wrote from the Roman jail, he didn't hesitate to recall the way of life he had once enjoyed and pursued. Nor did he deny that he had enjoyed some of those benefits. "I have learned the secret of being well-fed and of going hungry," he said. There's the possibility that we will become so pious that we don't know how to rejoice in comfort and pleasure. One day when Teresa of Avila was enjoying a rare feast, a partridge that had been sent to her by a well-wisher, she was rebuked by someone who was glad to find fault in her. Teresa replied, "There is a time for partridge and a time for penance." One should never become so taken with rain and cold that one despises the sunshine. I recognize that this is not a hazard for most of us, but all virtues have their dark side and we need to be on guard lest our righteousness become snickery self-righteousness.

And of course there's a sense in which the days of sunshine form the context for singing in the rain. One of my seminary professors, Dr. Don Holter—later a bishop in the United Methodist Church—was a prisoner of war during World War II, along with a number of other missionaries to the Philippines. Their daily ration of food was utterly minimal. During such deprivation, Dr. Holter said, one of their favorite social entertainments was to plan sumptuous imaginary banquets. They drew on all of their culinary memories and more in order to spread their dream tables—all the while laughing at their current circumstances. When first Dr. Holter told some of us of this game, I wondered. But the longer I thought about it, the more I realized its holy wisdom. As they recalled days of sunshine (including even imaginary ones!), these captive missionaries had a context for falling in love with their rainy days.

Most of us do this better after the rainy days are past. When old university or seminary classmates get together, they love to recall rainy days: the restaurant that included a free dessert with dinner on Tuesday evenings, the Thanksgiving dinner that featured Spam decorated with three cloves, the apartment so small that if you had dinner guests they got the two chairs and you and your spouse sat on a sofa pulled up to the table, how you prayed that a check would come before the major bill did. Such memories are entrees at reunion parties. But this isn't what I have in mind when I speak of falling in love with rainy days.

Nor am I willing to settle for the long view. I'll get to that later. But first I want us to look at right-now, this day that we didn't choose. At such times some earnest people decide that they must be out of the will of God, else something this bad wouldn't be happening to them. Believe me, our present level of pain or pleasure has virtually nothing to do with God's will. The Children of Israel had experienced the miracle of their escape from Egypt, but after only a short time on the road to their new home they decided they were better off as slaves in Egypt, where they "ate our fill of bread" (Exodus 16:3). Their location wasn't out of the will of God, but their attitude was.

The apostle Paul handled such matters better. He received a vision that he was to go into Macedonia with the good news of Christ. But in his first major stop, at Philippi, he and Silas were thrown into prison. Clearly, this didn't convince them that they were out of God's will in their Macedonian campaign. Thus after being flogged and locked "in the innermost cell and fastened . . . in the stocks" (Acts 16:24), about midnight they began to sing. I would call this "singing in the rain"; and I submit that if their feet hadn't been in stocks they might have competed with Gene Kelly's iconic dance.

I repeat: our circumstances of good or ill have little to do with the will of God, and thinking about the will of God is likely simply to distract us from taking care of the present. Our business is to deal with where we are. If this calls for repentance, then let us repent. For sure, it calls for a declaration of faith, a voice that says, "You know, O Lord, where I am and how I got here. Some of it can be attributed to circumstances beyond my control, and some of it to my own errors, whether recent or ancient. But just now my only business is to deal with where I am and to learn how to love this until you lead me somewhere else."

I don't believe in giving the present to despair while pining my heart away for the future. I don't believe in ceding this hour to the devil while I ask God for tomorrow. This hour, this circumstance, this place belongs to God, and I must take it conquest for God. How do I know that this circumstance belongs to God? Because I belong to God, and because *you* belong to God. Circumstances are peripheral compared to people. God works with people, people like you and me, and we then go to work on the circumstances. We fall in love with our rainy days.

God is indeed the God of the future, and by grace we get the long view of life. But I think it's a sin to wish away the present. It's so easy to do, you know. When we're waiting for Christmas, or a wedding day, or commencement, or a vacation trip, we can easily wish our lives away. These days between now and a calendar high point are God's days as surely as the day we've circled on the calendar, and there's something irreverent or ungrateful about wishing away God-given days.

I had to deal with this matter several years ago. I was asked to take on a job that I didn't want but which I knew I must accept. When I accepted the position, the terminal date was just over twenty months away (as it turned out, I held the position for nearly three years). During the first fifteen months I could tell you at any point how many months, weeks, and days remained on my assignment. But though I was counting off the days, my assignment was not a sentence. It was a calling, and I promised God and myself and my wife that I would enjoy every day of it. And I did. Some days I had to laugh in the face of the devil to do so, but I did.

And every day I was sustained by prayers. I prayed for myself, of course. But the best thing I knew was the blessing I was receiving from the prayers of other people. The prayers of kind people were building the roads down which I traveled each day.

And then there is the future. Every good farmer knows that rain is the down payment on the future. Rain may postpone a ball game for the farmer's son or daughter, and rain may delay planting a crop or some day of nurturing what has been planted. But rain is the farmer's future and the soil's friend.

Every metaphor has its limits, however, and surely this

is true of the metaphor of this chapter. Any farmer can also tell us that too much rain at the wrong time can delay planting until it's too late, or can destroy the harvest. And someone reading this will tell me that in your life there have been so many rainy days, so many Johnstown floods, that not much of life is left.

I won't insult you or your pain by any silly aphorism—the kind that sounds good when you don't hurt. I've had some pain in my life, but nothing to compare with pain I've seen in the lives of others, so I'm not about to say too much to someone whose road has been much harder than mine. I can say that I've known some of those people whose lives have been fiercely constricted by sickness, rejection, or defeat who could bring their testimony forward just now in favor of rainy days. And of course I could go back to words I quoted earlier in this chapter, from the apostle Paul. He had learned the secret, he said, "of being well-fed and of going hungry, of having plenty and of being in need" (Philippians 4:12). In particular he had known rejection by old friends and new, of betrayals, of life perils, and of a variety of physical punishments and torments. And to top it all, he was at that moment writing from prison. Paul's words were a testimony of experience, not a document of theory.

I postponed talking about the future until we had discussed the right-now. It is in the now that we learn to fall in love with rainy days—and in which, then, we become more fully equipped for dealing with the future. Rainy days, rightly employed, put the rest of life's weather in perspective. When we face another storm or perhaps simply some heavy clouds, we know that we've lived through worse. I am part of that generation that grew up during the Great Depression and the political insanity of Hitler, Mussolini, and Stalin. Our hymns and sermons and prayers and faith that were sufficient for those days provide perspective for anything that has since come to pass. Or that could yet happen.

Especially and particularly, I have come to know the

faithfulness of God. The apostle Paul didn't conclude his testimony with the words I quoted above regarding "well-fed and hungry." He went on to tell his secret: "I can do all things through him who strengthens me" (Philippians 4:13). Paul was not an apostle of ancient stoicism or of modern stiff-upper-lip. He had strength beyond the philosophy he had learned from the Greeks and the Romans and the theology he had gotten from even the great Hebrew prophets. He knew a source, a person, the Lord Christ. Christ had accompanied him into the Philippian jail, through endless persecutions and betrayals. Christ had taught him to fall in love with rainy days.

I am certainly not a fatalist. If anything, I'm too easily an optimist. But my optimism has a very real foundation in my faith in Christ. And because I have lived all my life with the Bible, I am a realist. I know that life has its varieties— or to use the common term, its ups and downs. So my lessons in life include this counsel to fall in love with our rainy days. I know there will be rainy days—for you and for me and for everyone. It is written into the dailyness of life's experience as surely as it is written into the fruitfulness of nature: there *are* rainy days, and they work wonderfully well in the whole economy of life. As I understand it, we won't escape rainy days until we get to heaven, because on this earth we can't survive without them. In heaven, I'm told, you and I will be perfect, which means that we won't need contrast in order to recognize beauty.

Until then, we'll need rainy days. And we'll get them. The secret therefore is simple. Learn to embrace them, and before you know it, they will hug you in return.

NOTES

1. Thomas Friedman, "At 59, Tom Watson still teaching us life's lessons," *Lexington Herald Leader*, 7-31-09, page A 11.
2. Frederick Buechner, *Listening to Your Life* (San Francisco: HarperSanFrancisco, 1992), 18.

CHAPTER 8

A Friend Is a Friend Is a Friend

Casey Stengel led the New York Yankees to seven world championships, which demonstrates that he knew baseball pretty well. Some of us remember him also as a philosopher. We didn't always know what he meant, but the same can be said for several philosophers, so in this regard Mr. Stengel is not exceptional. He said memorably, "There comes a time in every man's life, and I've had many of them."

I think I know what he meant but I'm not sure, and I couldn't explain it even if I were more certain. But it applies to what I want to say just now about friends. I cherish friends, and I think I always have. This is one of the evidences that I'm normal. We humans were made for friendship. I feel, as I look back on what already is a long life, that I've had more than my share of friends. I can recall the earliest from experiences and events before kindergarten, though without names, but I can bring back scores of names beginning in the fourth, fifth, and sixth grades and hundreds since then. When I fumble now to bring up a name that should be on the tip of my tongue, I want to tell the patient listener, "If your encyclopedia of names was as extended as mine, you too would find it hard to pull up a particular individual."

I thank God for all of these friends. Perhaps by now I've offended you by my use of the word *friend*, because I've made it seem commonplace, and you may hold to a sacred definition, as in the book of Proverbs: "A friend loves at all times" (Proverbs 17:17), and "a true friend sticks closer than one's nearest kin" (Proverbs 18:24). And I agree readily and vigorously that this is what most of us have in mind as the ultimate definition when we speak of friends. But the writer of Proverbs was wise enough to know that "friend" has a broad definition, so he prefaces the "true friend" by warning us, "Some friends play at friendship" (18:24).

That's something of what I have in mind when I say, "A friend is a friend is a friend." By this broader definition I've had a great many friends, covering an astonishing range in length, depth, and quality—and I suspect the same is true for you. In my imperfect way I'm trying to say that I agree with John Donne: "Any man's death diminishes me, because I am involved in Mankinde." The great poet-preacher was saying that our friendship includes the whole human race, even if we don't choose for it to be so. To be human is to need friends. To be human is to have a variety of friends. To be human is to be blessed with friends who merit the highest definition, and to be human is to have friends who deserve a more cautious definition. And it is human, too, to expect too much of our friends and to be disappointed—sometimes even heartbroken—that some haven't measured up to our expectations. And if we're wise we will realize that others have been disappointed in us as friends, and sometimes with substantial reason.

When Dr. Timothy Johnson, longtime medical correspondent on *ABC News*, summarized the secrets of a long and happy life, he said that one of the six secrets for having a healthy body and a healthy soul is to have friends. Loneliness, Dr. Johnson says, is "the most devastating disorder in our society." He marvels that so many people, even successful people, don't have close friends. So the first treatment Dr. Johnson recommends to people who are dealing with anxiety is "to get together with a good friend."[1]

But suppose you don't have a good friend; where do you find one? Or suppose you've had a great friend, and the friend has died or moved or—well, somehow the friendship has just fallen to pieces. Where do you go from here? Conventional wisdom recommends that you join some organization, especially a church or a synagogue, and this is good counsel. As a pastor for nearly forty years, I've seen it work in literally hundreds of cases. But it isn't foolproof, because friendship isn't a rocket science. Actually, it's much more complicated. The human psyche has so many moving parts that it's hard to predict how two persons will mesh in the strange combination of personality, spirit, intellect, and general taste that go into friendship. Sometimes, ironically, it is a person's very need of friendship that frightens off potential friends.

So sometimes we'd be wise to settle for an acquaintance type of friendship—remember, "a friend is a friend is a friend"—rather than looking for a friend who will stick closer than family. In time some ordinary friendships grow into the storybook kind. A great many years ago I became pastor of a downtown church in a wonderful city at the same time an acquaintance moved into the pastorate of a neighborhood church. A wise church official who knew us both smiled: "It will be interesting to see how you two get along in the same town," he said. I figured we'd probably get along at a distance. A fairly long distance.

But as time went by, we came to enjoy one another more and more. Our luncheon meetings became more frequent. Occasionally we were competitors, but it didn't seem to matter. Eventually we became very, very good friends. At a time when I needed a quality friend the most, he was there. A friend is a friend is a friend. You never know when an absolute gem will come your way. They're rarely prefaced by trumpets and drums. But they do require a certain amount of nurturing and a good measure of trust. You have to suspend disbelief at times, and be forgiving when something in you is unduly critical. Very few friendships—especially in their adolescent period—can survive harsh criticism.

And don't be surprised if at some point in a friendship one party prizes the friendship more than the other. I think that only rarely do friendships grow at the same speed and intensity. Pay attention to the signs, but not too much attention. That is, don't keep taking the pulse of a friendship. Attend to it, but don't hover.

Adela Rogers St. John, the brilliant newspaperwoman and screenwriter of the early- and mid-twentieth century, had an interesting rule. I'm quoting it from memory, but I think I have it pretty much as she spoke it: "Choose your friends for their faults. Their virtues will take care of themselves." That is, find people whose faults you can live with. This implies, of course, that everyone has faults, so if you were planning on a friend with measured perfection, you can abandon that idea before going further.

But some faults drive us to distraction, while others we can manage. And there's not necessarily any logic to the power of these faults. As a pastor I've counseled with persons who have been able to look past infidelity in a partner, a fault that many would consider ultimate, while being unable to bear with some much smaller matter. I have an idea that many of us employ Ms. St. John's theory without knowing we're doing so: that is, we eliminate some possible friendships before they even get a start and we don't know we've done so, let alone why we've done so. Realizing it or not, we've decided that some particular quality or manner in a given person irritates us enough that we never consider the person further, and probably avoid further contact.

I think often of Israel's great King David, and of his capacity for friendship—and then of the friendship void which must have marked his later life, and what that void may have meant for his spiritual and professional welfare. The Bible portrays David as a person with great capacity for human relationships—and indeed, for the divine friendship, too, for here was a person who surely loved God and who in turn was a person after God's own heart. David's friendship with Jonathan is one of the most storied relationships in all of literature, both sacred and secular. Jonathan, heir to the throne of his father, King Saul, and in every sense worthy of the position, protected David from assassination, knowing that by doing so he was making it possible for David to become Israel's king. The biblical historian says of the two men that they loved each other more than they loved their own lives.

David seems to have had the gift of friendship, a gift he exercised at many levels. When he was exiled from Israel, he drew to himself a collection of rough ne'er-do-wells—persons whose loyalty needed to be bought anew daily. He held this disparate group together. This is an extension of the gift of friendship into the ability of leadership. As Israel's warrior king, he was obviously adored by his soldiers, from rank and file to generals. And when late in his life his son Absalom turned against him and mounted an effective revolt, David was able still to hold the loyalty of key military, religious, and administrative leaders and to regain the throne.

But David's later life was marred by several serious failures, especially the adultery with Bathsheba and the ensuing murder of her husband, Uriah, and David's numbering of the people in an act of political and personal arrogance. Let me speculate, though of course I have no proof. If in later life David had found a friend of Jonathan's stature and devotion, I wonder if David might have been spared those errors of judgment, those egregious sins. Suppose there had been someone close enough to David that David would have confided in him that he had seen Bathsheba bathing—a beautiful sight!—and that he was drawn to her. And suppose this trusted soul had answered, "Friend, you can't play this game. You can't sin against God and Bathsheba and Uriah. You dare not, absolutely dare not." And suppose, when David wanted to number Israel, if there had been a friend of Jonathan's stature who could have clapped him on the shoulder and said, "Don't be a fool. You don't need any more accolades or proofs of importance. This kind of deed is beneath you. Cut it off!"

Just suppose David had had such a friend. Just suppose he had found a successor to Jonathan.

Well, if you've never had even one Jonathan in your life—a friend willing to die for you—you'll tell me that David had enjoyed favors enough. Great friendships are scarce in the marketplace of life, and no one should ask for two when many people don't even get one. I agree. And you might also reason that it's easier to find a great friendship when one is young but that it can be nearly impossible for a person in a high position to do so. Corporate and institutional and political leaders know that good friends are very hard to come by. You never know how much a given person can be trusted, or whether people are drawn to you more by your role than by your person. I can see all kinds of reasons why David never got another friend like Jonathan. Perhaps he himself closed the door to any such possibility. Nevertheless, I ask myself what might have happened if David had had another great friend.

The early Methodist movement built in a structure for friendship—spiritual friendship, with covenanted commitments. It began with Charles Wesley and fellow scholars at Oxford, then included Charles's older brother, John. The members of this fellowship pledged themselves to God and to each other, so that they were willing to subject themselves to mutual interrogation and soul-baring. The standards they set for themselves would frighten away any but the most earnest.

Some years later, as the Methodist revival swept through the British Isles, these small covenant groups were the key element for spiritual growth. They were the secret of a spiritual revival that maintained its integrity longer than perhaps any such spiritual renewal in Christian history. It was a kind of organized friendship, but it worked. Its success depended largely on the spiritual hunger of its participants. And of course its focus was on Christ rather than on the individual loyalties within the group. I suspect that the success of each group depended on their loving the group and loving one another within the group more than on their particular one-on-one bonds. But without a doubt it provided a setting for a special kind of friendship, and it produced a great host of saints.

And while I am cautious about organizing friendships—because as I said earlier, the qualities that go into great friendships are exceedingly complicated—I nevertheless believe that structures can provide a setting where friendships can grow. And I remind you again that a friend is a friend is a friend. Friends come in many shapes and sizes, and while their quality may differ, each one deserves care and honor.

Most of what I've said thus far has been subjective, as if the value of friendship is in the benefits we receive. Anyone who goes after friendship in such a mood will miss it entirely because of course the essence of friendship is in its emphasis on the other person and in the mutuality of sharing. I have known persons, as have you, who are passionate in their hunger for friendship but who quite unconsciously weigh it largely on the scale of their own benefit.

So let us ponder how we can be a friend, which brings us back to the matter of "a friend is a friend is a friend." We can't be an intimate friend or a best friend to everyone, but we can cast a wide net of friendship if we're willing to invest energy in its various forms. Perhaps the most significant continuing expression of friendship is the gift of undivided attention. This is a gift we can extend at every level of friendship. It isn't restricted to that poignant hour when a cherished friend is pouring out his or her soul. We can—and should—give the same fullness of listening when we're talking with the person checking our garments at the cleaning establishment or in a moment of generally mundane conversation at a social occasion.

The subject matter doesn't have to be profound. In most conversations, it is not. But the attention should be complete. Few things are more diminishing to a person than the realization that the other person is only partly present. You don't know if they're waiting to talk with someone else, or whether they're simply preoccupied—but you know quite well that you aren't the object of their attention or their emotional energy.

So whatever the level of conversation, give it your attention. If it is small talk, try to develop some originality in your small talk rather than settling for clichés. If the greeting is routine, be sure that your response is delivered with the kind of smile and personal involvement that lifts the routine to quite another level. If it's only a thirty-second conversation, give it your self for those thirty seconds. A friend is a friend is a friend. This friendship at the checkout counter is not the stuff of David and Jonathan, but nevertheless you can bring to it a quality of attention that will cause the person to report the incident to their spouse that evening.

Well, to paraphrase Casey Stengel, "There comes a friend to every person's life, and I've had many of them." I urge you to remember that *friend* is a word of such proportions that it is compelled to keep company with all sorts of adjectives—close, long-time, casual, best, wonderful, disappointing, ordinary, faithful, once-in-a-lifetime—well, you choose the word or supply one of your own. But respect the fact that after you've looked at all those defining, modifying terms, a friend is a friend is a friend, and they all have their place in the human story. Further, we ought, all of us, to try to fill as many of those definitions as possible for other human beings.

And every day while you're thanking God for life and breath and beauty, thank God for friends, whatever their shape or size or definition. And thank God for the chance to be a friend to someone else. And don't sell short any level of friendship. Because a friend is a friend is a friend.

NOTE

1. Timothy Johnson, M.D., "Have a Long and Happy Life," *Guideposts,* September, 2004, 35.

CHAPTER 9

Get a GOOD Night's Sleep

I'm always fascinated by the statistical studies that reveal how you and I spend the years of our lives. The figures are sometimes quite unbelievable and for that reason, quite appalling. A study several years ago reported that we invest six years of our lives eating, which seems to suggest more leisurely meals (a good idea, on the whole) than most people practice in this fast food, buy-in-the-drive-through world. Another study reported that we spend six years standing in line—check-out counters, theaters, sporting events, and airports. Personally, I've concluded that if we add up all of the data from such studies, the total would make centenarians of all of us.

But let me give you a statistic that's pretty easy to prove. If a person lives to be seventy years old (which is below the current life expectancy in most of the Western world), we'll spend more than a third of the years sleeping—roughly twenty-four years. Rip Van Winkle had nothing on us, except that he crowded twenty years into one long nap.

You can see where I got my figures. The general standard for a night's rest is eight hours, though some of us have rarely had such a pattern in our adult lives. But then there are also cat naps, Sunday afternoon naps, and those occasions when we sleep in settings where we're supposed to be awake. And of course in our infancy and early childhood we sleep a great deal more than eight hours a night. So put it all together and it's easy to see that we spend a third of our lives sleeping. Twenty-three or twenty-four years, at a minimum. That's a lot of shut-eye.

But even as I give you that data, I hear someone making a rebuttal. You want to tell me that some people may be spending a third of their time sleeping, but that you haven't had a good night's sleep in years. Or someone else reminds me of the hundreds of millions of dollars that Americans spend on sleeping pills of one kind or another, both over-the-counter and prescription. Cervantes tells us, in *Don Quixote*, that sleep is "the balance and weight that equalizes the shepherd and the king, the simpleton and the sage." But those who struggle to find sleep, including those who see their sleeplessness as a kind of badge of distinction, will contend there's nothing equalizing about sleep, because they never get their share. Our parents and grandparents—probably going back to Eden—have agreed on a simple statement of wisdom: "There's nothing like a good night's sleep." And regardless of whether such sleep is common or uncommon for you, you'll probably agree.

But how do you get such sleep? Some say, "If you're tired enough, you'll fall asleep." But a common phrase in our speech argues otherwise: "Last night I was just too tired to fall asleep." So we humans have developed our sleep-secrets. The proverbial one is counting sheep. I wonder if anyone still does so. And I wonder how the idea started? Obviously the phrase comes out of a simpler time, an agricultural world, but people who can't remember when they last saw a sheep still use the term.

Anne Fadiman reminds us that for some time the novelist F. Scott Fitzgerald put himself to sleep by a fantasy in which he was the Princeton quarterback leading his team to victories over Yale. Anne's father, the literary critic Clifton Fadiman, had his own remarkable games for falling asleep. The most fascinating, in my judgment, was called "I Shook

Hands with Shakespeare." Fadiman had shaken hands with Cornelia Otis Skinner, who had no doubt shaken hands with her father, Otis Skinner, who had shaken hands with Edwin Booth—and so on, back to Shakespeare. I think it's a lovely game, but it calls for more knowledge than I possess. Besides, I'm afraid if I got too far into my quest I'd have to get out of bed to start consulting the encyclopedia.

On the whole, I fall asleep rather easily. But when I can't, my secret is one I gladly recommend. I pray for persons, by name, beginning with my immediate family and moving then to whatever names come to mind. This is a healthy exercise. It turns my mind toward God and toward others, thus away from myself. Thinking about one's self is particularly opposed to sleep, of course, and the best way to avoid thinking about self is to think about others. When I pray for others, I mention not only the name, but something specific about the person, whether by way of gratitude or petition. Sometimes I think of someone whose name I can't bring to the surface of my mind. In such instances, I describe the person to God—"You know who I mean, dear Lord"—and trust the divine computer system.

All of which brings me to the heart of this discussion. I believe that sleep is one of God's good gifts and that it is God's intention that we should enjoy it—every one of us. I believe, further, that the simple phrase "a *good* night's sleep" has more significance than we realize. God is good, and day and night are good, and sleep is good. We are on the side of goodness when we seek to sleep; we're following the pattern of creation.

Obviously with this as with all other rules there are exceptions to what I'm saying: there are times, for instance, when we ought to make something right before even trying to sleep. There is sometimes a letter to be written, a telephone call to be made, or an e-mail sent. And we do well to remember the apostle's warning, "do not let the sun go down on your anger," and the phrase that follows it, "and do not make room for the devil" (Ephesians 4:26-27).

Anger, resentment, thoughts of revenge, worry—all of these are exceedingly bad bedtime companions.

Which brings us back to some inherent wisdom in the creation story. "And there was evening and there was morning, the first day," Genesis declares (1:5); and so through the continuing days, always this pattern that seems to us counter-structured: "evening and morning." We think of our days as morning to evening. But as the Hebrew Scriptures portray it, Monday begins, not when I arise on Monday morning, but when I go to bed Sunday evening. And see the wisdom this implies. If I take a collection of worry, anger, or even of busy planning to bed with me, I'm making a poor start for the next day. Not only will I delay my falling asleep, I'm likely to poison my sleep with elements that will destroy sleep's effectiveness. When we retire at night, we chart the emotional and spiritual course of the next day by the stuff we take to bed with us.

William Quayle was one of Methodism's most colorful bishops. He often recalled a night when he was especially concerned about several of his churches and pastors. He tossed, turned, and struggled until it seemed to him that the Lord said, "Bill, you go to sleep and I'll stay up and worry for the rest of the night." I think God's loving Spirit would say something like that to many of us when we're frustrating the purpose of the bed on which we lie and the hours we intend to rest. Victor Hugo, the iconic French novelist, urged that we have courage for the great sorrows of life and patience for the small ones; and when a day's work and its tasks are done, to go to sleep in peace, remembering that God is awake.

The creation story puts a holy premium on rest. It declares that God chose after six days of creation-work to rest and enjoy what had been done. Each night's rest, it seems to me, ought to have something of this same quality. We have finished a day's work. Now it is time to lay it aside, with gratitude, and to feel God's smile of approval. Has the day been a failure in some way? If so, is there anything substantive that I can still do about it? If not, put that concern to bed, but not in your bed; put it elsewhere, so it doesn't pester you during the night. Then meet it with new vigor in the morning. If there's anything at the end of Tuesday that can still be remedied as the day winds down, do it. But don't let Tuesday evening—the emotional and spiritual beginning of Wednesday—intrude on your night's rest and on God's purposes for your new day.

And don't frustrate your search for *rest* by thinking too much about *sleep*. Jesse Stuart, the wise novelist, essayist, and poet of another generation, suffered a major heart attack that hospitalized him and immobilized him for weeks. At last a time came when he was allowed to walk a bit in his beloved Kentucky countryside. He lay down on a bed of old leaves. As he grew quiet "and when wild birds stopped singing and crows quit cawing and ground squirrels hushed their talking, I could hear the trickle of the little stream down the Byrnes Hollow. I had found the right bed for recovery, so much so that I hated for my period of afternoon rest to end. If I ever went to sleep, I was not conscious of it. There is a deeper rest than sleep, when the mind relaxes in complete harmony with the intimate, known world around it."[1]

I subscribe to Stuart's words about "a deeper rest than sleep." Some studies have demonstrated that lying quietly is just as restorative as actual sleep. If I'm going to take the proverbial power nap, I don't worry about falling asleep, I simply seek to relax. Almost always I fall asleep, even if only for five minutes. But I don't let the pursuit of sleep— as if the word itself were magic, as it seems to be for many people—to prevent my relaxing and resting. People sometimes refer to sleeping "restlessly," and then waking up more tired than when they went to bed. Perhaps it is better to rest sleeplessly than to sleep restlessly.

You and I need rest. We are wired for a balance between activity and rest, and if either gets out of proportion, our physical, mental, and spiritual health is in danger. We can't fool Mother Nature. The person who—perhaps for reasons beyond personal control—gets by with minimal rest is in fact mortgaging some part of his or her person. It may be the body, which will demand payment later in a hospital room, or it may be the nerves, which will exact their payment at the cost of the person's family or co-workers. Or it may be at a spiritual level, as the person struggles increasingly with depression, acedia, anxiety, or a sense of worthlessness. We are complex creatures, you and I, with our intricate inter-weavings of body, mind, and spirit, and our total person needs appointed quantities of rest.

But quantity alone isn't the answer. In rest, as in much of life, quality is also a factor. Which brings us back to our title-phrase: a *good* night's rest. Those devout souls who gave us the Psalms knew something about sleep. In one instance the writer is struggling with anger, which is a poor bedfellow. He prays, "In your anger do not sin; / when you are on your beds, / search your hearts and be silent" (Psalm 4:4 NIV). His method works. He concludes his poem-prayer in victory: "I will lie down and sleep in peace, / for you alone, O LORD, / make me dwell in safety" (Psalm 4:8 NIV).

Psalm 3 is traditionally said to have been written by David when he was fleeing from deep trouble. His son Absalom had revolted against him and had won several key personalities to his side. It is night, and the psalmist in flight is badly in need of rest. He recites his troubles to the Lord, then announces:

> I lie down and sleep;
>   I wake again, for the LORD sustains me.
> I am not afraid of ten thousands of people
>   who have set themselves against me all around.
> (Psalm 3:5-6)

I venture that literally thousands of soldiers have spoken these words or similar ones to God in fields of battle.

But there are other fields of peril for great numbers of people who live in urban settings where they barricade themselves behind triple-locked doors, protected by fire warning signals and special safety devices. And then there are those who awaken in fear of what our ancestors called those "long-leggedy beasties who go bump in the night." Real or imaginary, our fears can invade the hours when we need rest. We need the faith of the psalmist who, when the battle waited not far from his cave, could sleep. The Lord was with him; of that he was certain.

But there is far more to rest and to a good night's sleep than simply the restoring of our bodies and minds and spirits, wonderful as that blessing may be. Vast numbers of people have found that on occasion their minds find better solutions and more creative insights while they are sleeping than when they are intently at work. I have read such reports from poets, novelists, and philosophers. But I remember it also from a day as a nine-year-old when I was quietly sitting in on an adult conversation. My Uncle Sam, a man who knew farm machinery, told of a time when he had worked fruitlessly to repair an engine. It was hopeless. He decided to eat a late meal, forget it all, and go to bed. "But when I woke up the next morning," Uncle Sam said, "I knew just what to do. I couldn't wait to go out to the barn. In ten or fifteen minutes, I had the thing purring like a kitten."

I don't think Sam knew it, but David had a similar experience some three thousand years ago. "I bless the LORD who gives me counsel; / in the night also my heart instructs me" (Psalm 16:7). I wonder what the psalmist thought of during the night. The Bible tells several notable instances of persons to whom God spoke through dreams. Were some of those dreams partially a product of what the person had pondered before falling asleep? For example, was young Joseph thinking about his future, perhaps even comparing his talents and prospects with those of his brothers, on those nights when in his sleep he caught a divine insight about what would happen more than a decade later?

There's an uncertain line between taking mental stuff to bed that will keep us awake or that will cause us to toss restlessly in our sleep, and that kind of thinking that allows our minds to be beautifully productive during our hours of sleep. I can't give you a formula, and in truth I would be skeptical of anyone who did. I'm sure, however, that God is pleased to bless us in our sleep and that a significant secret lies in the role faith plays in our sleeping.

I'm thinking especially of another verse from the Psalms, a psalm attributed to Solomon. The writer is counseling against ventures where God is not consulted or brought into the partnership. It's vain to rise up early and stay up late, he says, for God "gives sleep to his beloved." A footnote gives another translation: "for he provides for his beloved during sleep" (Psalm 127:2). Whichever the translation, I like that word. I believe with the psalmist that we are among God's beloved and that we can therefore ask God for the gift of sleep—or on another hand, that God will provide for us as we sleep. What is it that you need most as you retire? Healing of body, perhaps, or relief from anxiety. Or deliverance from festering anger, anger we insist on nurturing because it gives us some ungodly pleasure even while it eats at the soul. And the power of worry needs to be broken for some, lest the soul become nothing more than a chewed-up bone. God gives sleep to his beloved, and provides for us even as we sleep.

Some years ago while traveling through several countries of Africa I learned of a custom that is common among some of the African people. If you greet them with a question that is common in our culture and in many parts of the world—"Did you sleep well last night?"—they graciously answer, "I did if you did."

It is a lovely word. So at this moment I wish you, under God, a *good* night's sleep. And if you get such sleep, I will sleep better, too.

NOTE

1. Jesse Stuart, *The Year of My Rebirth* (New York: McGraw-Hill Book Company, 1956), 107-8.

CHAPTER 10

Teach Us to Number Our Days

Iliked numbers in my grade school and junior high days, but it hasn't made an accountant of me. Like some of you, I postpone balancing my checkbook against the bank statement, and I sometimes wait too long before bringing together figures for my income tax report. But far worse, it is not until very recent years that I have enrolled in that fundamental accounting course, the one recommended by a wise poet several thousand years ago. Listen: "So teach us to number our days, that we may apply our hearts unto wisdom" (Psalm 90:12 KJV).

This is the most basic of all accounting—ultimately, the only arithmetic that really matters. The people to whom that great soul (traditionally said to be Moses) first addressed his words knew how to count their sheep, goats, and camels and from those figures to estimate how many of each they might have next year. And you and I, their twenty-first century descendants, do pretty well at totaling our stocks, bonds, and other holdings while also calculating our debts. But all these matters, even at their most important, are petty accounts. What really matters on this planet, for every one of us, above all else, is the number of years we get to spend here and what we do with those years. And while of course most of us don't know how many years or days we have left, we do know that sometime there will be an end to it all. With that fact in mind, we should do an accounting of our days so that when we've run out of time's funds, we will have used those funds to get what matters most.

Some years ago I knew a woman who was given an estimate of her days. Her doctor told her after a careful and extensive diagnosis that she had a year to live. That information would—to use a phrase—spook out some people. Not this great soul. By that time she had lived perhaps seventy-five years and was grateful to have had so many. She didn't think the doctor's word was in any way morbid. Rather, she found the information highly practical and decided to live accordingly. I don't remember her ever quoting Psalm 90, but she made its principle her own. She numbered her days, and did so with great wisdom.

As her pastor I called on her several times that year and saw her in her customary pew with her husband most Sundays. One day the family notified me that she was probably in her last week and that she would be glad for one more visit. I was more than glad to make it. We talked a few minutes about the general small stuff of the day, then got up to the big business.

"My doctor did me such a favor," she said, "when he told me I had just a year to live. And it looks as if his calculation was right. It's been a wonderful time. I've written all those letters that a person always plans to write and never gets around to. I've had a special visit with each of my grandchildren, knowing that it was to be our last visit, so I could tell them just what was on my mind, and they would hear it accordingly. I have prayed regularly and thoughtfully—I've always been faithful in prayer, you know, but in this year I've thought more about what I was saying when I prayed. As far as I can tell, I've taken care of everything and I'm ready to go."

She left on schedule. She was the kind of person who had used all of her years in a generally exemplary way, but her last year was wonderfully biblical. The psalmist would have said that she numbered her days, and did so with holy wisdom.

I was impressed by her experience and by the spirit in which she lived out her last year on earth. I thought about it often, at least in a general way. But I was between fifty-five and sixty years old at the time, and while I certainly was conscious of my mortality, I wasn't really thinking seriously about it. In the last few years, however, I have begun numbering my days, and now I ask myself why I didn't get an earlier start on this most basic of all accounting.

No, I don't know when I'm going to die. As a matter of fact, last week I received a report from my doctor following my physical exam in which he went through a rather long list of tests, all of which identified me as "normal." Years ago I wouldn't have felt complimented at being told I was "normal," but at this point in my life I receive it as high praise.

So I'm not numbering the days remaining to me, and I don't know how many there will be. But I *am* numbering some of what I hope to do in those days. I'm no longer going through the supermarket of life, grabbing from the shelves anything that momentarily strikes my fancy. Instead, I'm shopping my time with a list. Only occasionally do I throw something into my basket on a whim. Just often enough, I guess, to boast in my independence.

To begin with, I've been trying to settle some old accounts. I mean this in an entirely positive way. If I work at it, I can recall some people who have done me wrong, but I don't want to clutter my soul with such garbage. Nor do I plan to tell them I've forgiven them, because in most cases they don't think they ever were unjust, so my act of forgiveness would be rather self-serving and wouldn't help the other party at all. But I'm trying to make right those instances where I have hurt other people, whether intentionally or by some insensitivity on my part. As such instances come to mind, I'm working on them.

Second, I have a continuing list of thank-you names. As I have indicated earlier in this little book, I believe in gratitude and I've tried to keep my expressions of gratitude up-to-date. But now and again I think of someone I've overlooked (some elements of one's memory may deteriorate with age, but if the gratitude line improves, your soul is in good shape), and I try to hustle off a note. And sometimes I get a new take on an old gift, which makes me want to thank someone again: this later thought puts their kindness in an even more beautiful light.

And then there's my list of time-to and time-for. This is a living, changing project. I cross off things as I do them, but I think I'm adding new things faster than I complete old ones.

Take my reading list, for instance. I've bought hundreds of books in my lifetime, and I've read several. Now I am carefully weeding out books so I can concentrate on those I really want to read before I die. There is one book which I read every morning and have done so since I was eleven years old—my Bible. I keep reading it because I need it, and because it keeps reminding me of things I've forgotten and keeps revealing things I have been slow to see. But as for other books, I now have a list and I'm working on it with delight—and every time I finish one on the list, I find myself adding another or two. In one sense it's quite discouraging, but it's also very exciting.

I'd rather you didn't send me a title that you feel I really must read. Maybe you must read it, but I'm not you, so I want to choose what I will read. I urge you to make a list for yourself. Don't be ashamed to revise the list, and don't feel obligated to read something because you once put it on your list. You're changing and growing, and your list can change, too. But make a list, or else you'll waste one of life's surest gifts, the gift of reading. You'll discover that you've gone through many books and periodicals and that most of them haven't really mattered. Meanwhile, some truly wonderful mental excursions have gone unexperienced.

Which is to say—the world of books is rich beyond imagination, with variety enough to meet the tastes of every kind of reader. But the levels of quality also vary greatly, and it is nothing short of tragic to use precious reading hours in material that fails to touch something of our better nature. Find those books and authors that make your world larger and the presence of God more real. And this doesn't by any means suggest that a book is specifically religious. When the apostle Paul wanted to make a point with the philosophers on Mars Hill, he quoted not a Hebrew prophet but poets from within the company of the pagan philosophers. God is not without witness, even in unlikely places. Choose the best—that which will make you laugh and think and cry and grow.

And there's something to be said for offering a prayer as you begin to read. Many of us ask God's blessing on the food we eat—grateful that we have such, and hoping that it will nourish our bodies. Why not, then, give thanks to God for authors and editors and booksellers, and then a request that we will be nourished by what we read. If the food that goes into our stomachs calls for prayer, how much more the food that goes into our minds and souls.

And here's another list as you number your days: the places you'd like to see before you die. Several times during my years as a pastor I led tours, especially to lands of the Bible. So often older people, in the midst of their enjoyment, would express regrets—some that they had not made the trip while a spouse was still living, and others that they simply wished they had traveled when it was easier to get around. Start making your list now, and give it an order of priority and possibility. And don't be too quick to write something off as impossible. Your dreams may be more within your reach than you realize.

In the process of that list-making, don't forget the near-at-hand. I remind myself often of the wisdom of that crusty New England iconoclast, Henry David Thoreau. "I have traveled a good deal in Concord," he wrote. Concord was a small village, but there was more in its streets, its houses, and its people than most people ever imagined. I suspect that if we don't learn to travel a good deal in our hometowns, we won't find much in London or New York, either. Some people don't know as much about the city in which they live as does a perceptive tourist who becomes immersed in the city. If we'll learn to travel where we are, we'll see much more wherever we go.

But let me get closer to the heart of this accounting business. As we number our days, we ought especially to make time for people. Not as an obligation and not because they can benefit us, but simply because they are people. As such they are made in the image of God. And blurred as that image becomes in many lives, the image we find in people will help us most in our search for God. And they're interesting! Some are more obviously interesting than others, but sometimes those who at first sight seem rather dull or ordinary prove later to have depths to explore.

Many years ago, I spent one of my last days in Green Bay, Wisconsin, with two preacher friends. I suddenly realized how much I liked them both, and I became very sad that I hadn't spent more time with them when it would have been so easy to do so. And it slowly dawned on me that one must be intentional about friendship; one can't leave such a precious matter to chance. I believe it was that great twentieth-century Quaker Douglas Steere who urged that we put in our date books the "appointments" that really, really matter—time with our children still at home, our spouses, and our friends. The same can be said for writing or calling friends who are farther away. I still repent that I didn't keep in more frequent touch with my lifetime friend, Bill. True, he was an erratic correspondent, which meant that I might write several times before I would hear in return (though the length of his letters made up for the wait). But I should have made the time. As the wise Samuel Johnson said to Boswell, "A man, sir, should keep his friendship in a constant repair."

And Johnson spoke that word following another key fact: "If a man does not make new acquaintances as he advances through life, he will soon find himself left alone." As the years pass by, we lose friends to death. But long before that, we lose them by moving—theirs or ours. We don't intend to. "Let's keep in touch." "You'll always have a spare room at our house." "Don't forget to call or e-mail." But I turn again to that word, *intentional*. We have to move from having good intentions to becoming intentional. And I say all of this realizing that not every friendship has the elements to be deep or of extended length, and one shouldn't feel guilty that some friendships die a rather natural death. But they shouldn't die of careless neglect.

But above all, in this accounting of our years, keep time for God. Did you expect me to say that because I'm a preacher? It isn't the preacher in me that compels me; it's the needy soul in me. I have learned that I cannot live— really live!—without this divine friendship. So it is that I pray the penitent's prayer from Psalm 51: "Do not take your holy spirit from me" (Psalm 51:11). Whatever else I lose, not your friendship, dear God.

This friendship, too, must be intentional. The great saints sought for a constant sense of communion with God, but they began with set appointments—especially at the beginning of the day. Friendships are nurtured in the context of time, and the friendship with God is no exception to this rule.

Clergy who work in retirement communities or in places where there are many elderly sometimes joke about the good church attendance: "They're all cramming for finals." I don't think this is the case, at least not with many. Rather, people find more time for God when they're no longer under the pressure of their careers or the demands of a growing family or of professional social obligations. So they commune with God more—by their reading, their church attendance, their involvement in study groups, and in their service to others.

But it's a shame they wait so long. If this is the best and most rewarding way to live, why not follow it early? A song that was once standard in youth gatherings urged, "Give of your best to the Master; / Give of the strength of your youth."[1] The mood is right, for God's sake and for our own. If we want the divine friendship to have its full wonder at some later date, the time to begin is now.

All of which brings me around to noting that this counsel, "Teach us to number our days," is good for any age but it is best for the very young. But of course the young can rarely hear well. As we grow older, our auditory equipment deteriorates, but when we're young, our attentive, perceptive hearing is often poor. Frederick Buechner points out that "there is always the temptation to believe that we have all the time in the world, whereas the truth of it is that we do not." Rather, Buechner says, "for each of us there comes a point of no return."[2]

That sounds quite dismal; indeed, threatening. That's because it is. And that's the whole point of this business of being a good accountant. If people lose their savings, there's usually a chance they can recover part of what they've lost, and sometimes more. So, too, with a career; biographies are packed full of such stories.

But time is another matter. We don't all get the same number of years, but it's our business to use what we have, and I suspect that isn't inappropriate to think when reading Jesus' parable of the talents that the key element is time itself—and that God will judge us for what we do with the time we have. There's a better chance that we will use our time well if we come to realize that time is sacred. It is our only measure on this earth for what eternity means, and if we don't use it well here, how dare we think we have a right to eternity?

Moses was right: "So teach us to count our days / that we may gain a wise heart" (Psalm 90:12). Here is a first lesson in wisdom: Become a good accountant of the only irreplaceable gift. Time. Days. Hours.

Now.

NOTES

1. Howard B. Grose, "Give of Your Best to the Master," *Favorite Hymns of Praise* (Chicago: Tabernacle Publishing Company, 1972), 348.

2. Frederick Buechner, *Listening to Your Life* (San Francisco: Harper-SanFrancisco, 1992), 138.

CHAPTER 11

If You See It, You Can Have It

A great many years ago—specifically, when I was still
in my twenties—I heard a sermon that is with me
still today. The preacher was a middle-aged woman,
a truly remarkable human being. She had felt the call to
preach as a young mother and homemaker. She had no professional education; I don't know that she was even a high
school graduate. She had few if any role models; the idea of
women in ordained ministry was still thirty or forty years
away. But by the time I knew her she was already something of a legend, pastor of a large, metropolitan congregation that had grown out of a gathering that had begun in
her own living room.

She preached that day from the Old Testament story of
Elijah and Elisha. I remember the sermon only for its text
and the phrase that ran through the sermon. The phrase
worked like a motif in a symphony, at first quietly from the
flutes, then insistently from trombones, and at last in a kind
of raucous laughter from full tympani: *If you see it, you can
have it.* I can hear it still, just as I have heard it in my soul
through these many decades, and just as I have heard myself repeat it to some of my students in these later years of
my teaching.

Let me remind you of the biblical story that gave birth

to her sermon. Elijah was the first great prophet of Israel, after Moses. He was a dramatic figure, destined to an iconic role. There were schools of the prophets in his day—we would call them theological seminaries today, or perhaps professional organizations. Apparently Elijah belonged to none of them but was held in fearful reverence by them all. At a crucial time in Elijah's ministry, God instructed him to enlist a young farmer named Elisha, whom he could mentor to be his successor.

Now it was time for the end of Elijah's ministry. Apparently everyone sensed it, because as Elijah came successively to schools of the prophets in Bethel and Jericho, the prophets said to Elisha, "Do you know that today the LORD will take your master away from you?" In each instance Elisha answered, "Yes, I know; keep silent" (2 Kings 2:3). But more important and more painful, Elijah himself seemed to want to establish a distance between himself and his young associate. "Stay here," Elijah told him, at Gilgal, Bethel, and Jericho, but Elisha refused to stay behind.

Unable to shake the tenacious young man, Elijah said, "Tell me what I may do for you, before I am taken from you." Elisha, audacious, said, "Please let me inherit a double share of your spirit." Elijah answered, "You have asked a hard thing; yet, if you see me as I am being taken from you, it will be granted you; if not, it will not" (2 Kings 2:9-10).

A hard thing, indeed. Shall a violin student say to Itzhak Perlman, "I intend to be twice the concert artist you are"? Or shall a high school math student say to Albert Einstein, "I hope by my studies to put your discoveries into the shade"? We might admire the optimism of a young person who would voice such a dream, but we'd also agree that they had no idea what they were saying. I wish I knew all that was in Elijah's mind when he answered Elisha, "You have asked a hard thing." A thousand memories may have crossed Elijah's mind, to be summarized in a sentence: "You have no idea the price I've paid for the work God has given me to do."

But as crusty and impatient as Elijah could sometimes be, he didn't stop by telling the young farmer that his request was a difficult one. He told him how his request could be fulfilled. "If you see me as I am being taken from you, it will be granted you; if not, it will not." The preacher to whom I have referred recast Elijah's words into her theme sentence: *"If you see it, you can have it."*

As I have already said, I don't remember the details of the sermon. But I suspect the idea was something like this. Elijah was telling Elisha that he would have to care enough to persevere to the end. He wouldn't dare let anyone—including even Elijah—persuade him to turn back. And by that passionate commitment to your goal, you will be able to apprehend it. If you see it, you can have it.

Here is the first step toward any truly great achieving in life, any really worthwhile accomplishment. You must first of all be so convinced of its worth that you will pursue it even though everyone tells you you're on a hopeless quest. The other young prophets sensed that Elijah's ministry was near its end, and they were forceful in telling Elisha that his master was soon leaving—that is, "You're wasting your time staying with the master now, because he's about to be taken from you." Elijah himself seemed to offer the same counsel: there's no future in staying with me. Elisha had to believe so fully and so purely in his vision that he would hold to the hope that if he stayed with Elijah he would learn the secret of the prophet's magnificent power. You have to believe in the worth of the goal on which you have set your heart, and you have to believe in it passionately. A logical conclusion isn't enough, though it's nice when logic is on your side. And secondary matters, like the prospect of success or recognition, don't matter at all. The belief and its accompanying hunger must go deeper than that.

Isn't this, after all, what Jesus had in mind when he told the secret of the kingdom of heaven? My kingdom, Jesus said, is like a merchant who has found a pearl of supreme value: "He went and sold all that he had and bought it" (Matthew 13:45-46). Quite literally, you sell out to your dream, your vision. It is this vision that drove on Jesus' disciples. When a number of Jesus' followers began to leave him, Jesus asked the twelve, "Do you also wish to go away?" Peter answered, "Lord, to whom can we go? You have the words of eternal life" (John 6:67-68).

But we have to *see* it before we're ready to make such a commitment. And if we see it, we can have it.

There's no magic involved in this. And while my emphasis concentrates on the highest of all issues, our relationship to God, the basic principle works in all of life. Last week a rookie pitched his first game in the big leagues, and won. After the game he told reporters that he had dreamed of this day since before he was in kindergarten. Every young baseball fan has probably had such a dream, but for this young man it was a dream that wouldn't go away. He saw beyond what others could see—and because he saw it, he got it.

True as this word is as a positive principle, it also works in the negative. Thus Job tells his friends after his world has caved in, "Truly the thing that I fear comes upon me, / and what I dread befalls me" (Job 3:25). As I read Job's words, I wonder what fears slipped into Job's mind back in the time when his family was intact, his stock holdings so substantial, his health apparently perfect, and his standing in the community without comparison: How is it that he could fear when everything was going his way? And did those fears play any part in what followed? Did they in any way contribute to the disasters that came later? I don't know about Job, but as a general principle I think we make ourselves susceptible to trouble when we "expect the worst."

But it's almost as bad to expect nothing or to expect little as to expect the worst. If we have no grand vision in life, no high mountain that our souls long to climb, we condemn ourselves to live in life's lowlands.

If the secret is in the seeing, we need to be very careful

about where we focus the eye of our souls. So many of the goals to which people give themselves aren't really worth the investment. Thus Jesus warned the crowds that they might gain the world but lose their souls—and what kind of gain would that be? Material possessions have some measure of satisfaction, but they aren't worth friendship or conscience or character. Public recognition is pleasant, but it is fickle, far more easily lost than gained. Success is so difficult to define that one had better be very sure of the definition before beginning to pay the price.

But whatever the goal, you must see it before you can get it. As a teacher I try to elevate the taste of my students. I want them to read fine literature so they can tell the difference between a classic and hammock reading. I want them to develop a taste for excellence. I think there's some overarching quality in excellence regardless of the field, so I want my students to observe quality in art, in music, and in character. And especially, of course, I encourage them to hear really fine preaching. I want them to know that there is something more to excellence than just "taste"—and that's a difficult idea to get across in a culture where reputations are so often developed not by quality but by a skillful public relations program. Elisha will never become like Elijah until he *sees* Elijah, sees his secret.

So now and again when a student writes in an evaluation of a classic sermon from another day, "I'd love to have that preacher's gift," I scribble on the side of the paper, "If you see it, you can have it." The first step in attaining excellence is to recognize excellence when we see it. Because if we never see it, or if our taste becomes so dulled by mediocrity that we have no sense of what is superior, we'll never have the taste to know what is worth seeking.

It isn't surprising that literature has its periods, in country after country, when several great writers appear. On the American scene, one thinks of the village of Concord, Massachusetts, when Emerson, Thoreau, Alcott, Hawthorne, and Melville were exchanging thoughts; or of the years in Oxford,

England, when the Inklings—especially C. S. Lewis, Charles Williams, and J. R. R. Tolkien—hiked and talked and ate and drank together. At which moment someone is saying, "I'd love to have sat in on some of those hours"—and I will answer, "Then read them now! Listen in on their visits by way of the essays, novels, notebooks, and poems they left behind until seeing, you have it."

Keep up with the present, but have a substantial knowledge of the past against which to compare it. "There were giants in the land in those days"—figures towering enough that their memory is with us still. Use them to give your mind and soul a standard for judging contemporaries with intelligence. Remember that in every generation there are persons who make a passing impression and disappear. And recognize that we live in a time which by its very nature—and indeed by its intentions—has us raise up persons whose achievements are fleeting and whose gifts are average, and who will soon be nothing more than a topic for conversation's trivial pursuit. And remember, too, that historians and students of literature, art, and music (and of sports and entertainment) have a way of demolishing or exalting heroes of the past. Develop some standards of taste and merit of your own. Because that which we admire is that, eventually, for which we strive. And if you see it, you can have it.

But again I hear a modifying voice. You remind me that even a passion for a silk purse won't cut it for a sow's ear. You have a feeling that I am building up some soul for a great letdown.

And of course you're right. So let me say a qualifying word or two. First, I remind myself and you of Robert Browning's words: "Ah, but a man's reach should exceed his grasp, / Or what's a heaven for?" Only rarely does an Elisha see more miracles than his Elijah, but every soul rises higher for having caught some measure of the Elijah vision. If dreaming and reading the sports page and memorizing statistics would have made a baseball player, I would now be in Cooperstown's Hall of Fame, while in truth I had a hard time keeping a position on the church softball team. We have to find our own area of promise. And—especially!—we need to find an area that is worth Elisha's commitment.

Let me make a case for a level of excellence that is rarely mentioned and rarely sought: saintliness. Not many people dream of being a saint. And here's a major reason why: most of us don't see enough saints, or don't even read enough stories of the saints. We haven't been exposed to enough bona fide examples of truly great souls, so we hardly know that there's such a possibility on earth's horizon. True, we hear about a Mother Teresa, but her way of life seems as far removed from ours as geographically India is removed from where we live. In truth it's rather safe to hold up Mother Teresa as a model since the context for her sainthood is so different from the structures of our lives.

But as a matter of fact, there are more saints out there than we are likely to realize. And perhaps, just perhaps, God would be pleased if you and I were to become the kind of persons who would inspire others to a more beautiful way of life. The saints are the true salt of the earth; they keep this planet of ours from rotting of its own misuses. True holiness is therefore the ultimate goal. But there's a hazard in seeking it. That is, if we seek holiness for our own satisfaction or our own sense of fulfillment, we'll never really get it. We seek holiness best when we are unselfconscious. This sounds pretty tricky, and I suspect that it is. As we seek God, however, and serve others, holiness is likely to take care of itself.

"If you see it, you can have it." The sentence can be applied at any and every level of life. A coach can make it his or her theme in the locker room talk before the biggest game of the season. A commencement speaker can use it to send off the graduating class. It can be the concluding word for the sales manager meeting with a group of hopeful, fearful college students who are setting out to sell encyclopedias door-to-door. A parent can post it on the mirror as a goal with which to begin each day.

But because the concept is so true, and because if rightly used it is so powerful, it should be used with care. The goal should be worthy, and the standard of measure should be true excellence. And at best, it should be seen under the judgment of eternity. Why see anything less? Why want anything else?

Because, if you see it you can have it. That's what the lady told me, and she got it from Elijah.

CHAPTER 12

Bring in God's Kingdom Every Day

We humans are dreamers. We love to imagine things that are bigger than we have ever experienced and then to begin planning how we'll bring them to pass—and sometimes we begin celebrating their fulfillment before we've made even one step toward any reality. Some of our dreams are outlandish; if they were accomplished, it would be to no purpose. Others are so self-centered and self-exalting that they reflect the worst in us rather than the best. Still others are beautiful: the stuff on which humanity's progress has been built. But dream, we will.

It comes with our genes. We can't help it. It's part of what it means to be human. I can't prove that animals don't dream, but it seems pretty evident that they don't try to better themselves—at least not until we humans decide that they will do so, to fulfill some of our purposes for them. The rest of creation seems to do what it was created to do: fish got to swim and birds got to fly, the popular song of another generation insisted; and we could add that trees got to leaf, and tides got to ebb and flow, and perennials have to return each year. But human beings? We have to dream, and with our dreams, change. Change ourselves, our environment, and the lives of those around us. Sometimes, it should be noted, against their will.

I'm not a scientist so I don't know if there's an evolutionary theory about this. Perhaps evolutionary thinking would reason that the very fact of our survival has been a result of our adapting and changing and keeping ahead of disaster, and therefore we keep changing because this has been our secret of survival. My understanding of who we humans are and how we function comes by way of a philosopher-theologian-poet, the writer of Genesis, who said that we are made in the image of God and that the breath of God is in us. God's breath is the essence of creativity, so it's instinctive for us humans to keep changing, keep dreaming, keep imagining. It is, I repeat, part of our genetic code.

Jesus came preaching a message that aimed directly at our capacity for dreaming. The Gospel of Mark puts it this way: "Jesus came to Galilee, proclaiming the good news of God, and saying, 'The time is fulfilled, and the kingdom of God has come near; repent, and believe in the good news' " (Mark 1:14-15).

The kingdom of God! Now there's a dream big enough to capture the energy of even the most adventuresome soul. Jesus not only taught and preached the kingdom, he brought it to pass. The sick, the poor, the rejected, and the lost were drawn to Jesus and to the hope he embodied. This was "the good news," Jesus said, that the kingdom of God had come near, and therefore Jesus invited all who would to "repent, and believe in the good news." Since "repent" means to turn around and go in the opposite direction, Jesus was saying, "Turn your back on the bad news and start following the good news—the news of the kingdom of God."

Jesus talked more about the kingdom of God than about any other single subject. It was the theme that ran all through his teaching and preaching and that dominated them. It seems clear that it was the flash word as far as his political/religious enemies were concerned. After all, to speak about another "kingdom" in the midst of an empire that controlled most of the then-known world was to ask for trouble. Thus when Jesus was crucified, the sign on the cross read, "King of the Jews." The sign was intended to mock the Jews, but it also declared the charge that had led to Jesus' crucifixion: he had campaigned for the kingdom of God, and they gave him a cross. Those who arranged for Jesus' crucifixion could never have imagined that twenty centuries later the cross would be the most widespread symbol in the world and the symbol of Jesus' kingdom.

After his resurrection Jesus continued to speak "about the kingdom of God" (Acts 1:3). And yet in the course of the discussion, when the disciples inquired, "Lord, is this the time when you will restore the kingdom to Israel?" Jesus answered, "It is not for you to know the times or periods that the Father has set by his own authority." Their business, he said, was to wait for the power of the Holy Spirit so they would be ready to be his witnesses in every corner of the world (Acts 1:6-8).

I can't blame the disciples for continuing to ask about the kingdom, because almost everything Jesus said about it was vague, sometimes to the point of seeming self-contradictory. He described the kingdom in parables and in figures of speech. His major campaign speech for the kingdom, the Sermon on the Mount, described how people would live in the kingdom, but not how the kingdom would come to pass or how it would be organized or administered. Its economic platform was nothing if not revolutionary: "Do not worry about your life, what you will eat or what you will drink, or about your body, what you will wear" (Matthew 6:25). This kind of language wouldn't go far on a twenty-first century political platform. And if a substantial portion of our country were to take such counsel seriously, the Dow Jones would quickly plunge to new depths. Jesus said nothing about national defense, but if his word about personal injury was applied to international affairs—"But if anyone strikes you on the right cheek, turn the other also" (Matthew 5:39)—well, who can imagine what would happen?

As I said a moment ago, Jesus began his ministry by declaring that the kingdom of God had "come near." In his Sermon on the Mount he said that the poor in spirit have the kingdom (Matthew 5:3). When a scribe, a sensitive religious leader, agreed that the law of God was summed up in loving God and loving our neighbor, Jesus commended him: "You are not far from the kingdom of God" (Mark 12:34). And when a group of Pharisees asked Jesus when the kingdom of God was coming, Jesus answered, "The kingdom of God is not coming with things that can be observed; nor will they say, 'Look, here it is!' or 'There it is!' For, in fact, the kingdom of God is among you"—or as the footnote translation has it, "within you" (Luke 17:20-21).

I could add a great deal more information to our discussion, because Jesus said so many things about the kingdom. But to do so would probably only lead to more discussion and general speculation—and I gather from reading the scriptures that the kingdom is more about action than about discussion. In fact one sometimes senses that discussing the kingdom is a good way to avoid doing anything about it.

So I proceed on what is quite clear. First, that the kingdom is of primary importance to Jesus. As I said earlier, it was his primary theme from the beginning of his public ministry to the closing meeting with his disciples. Second, the kingdom is described much of the time in personal terms, with virtually nothing said about how it is to be organized or how we are to bring it to pass. It "is not coming with things that can be observed," because it is something within us—perhaps I can dare to say, it is a state of mind or of heart, an attitude toward life, a controlling purpose and meaning. And yet I hesitate even as I write, because I fear I am only adding words to an already wordy discussion.

So, tired of discussion—especially the kind of discussion that can so easily take the place of action—I have come to a conclusion. I have decided that it is my business to do everything in my power, every day, to bring in the kingdom of heaven. I am convinced that there is nothing in our lives that is so small that it cannot further the kingdom. And at the same time, unfortunately, there's nothing so small that it cannot in some way delay or frustrate the kingdom. This realization is both exciting and frightening. It's exciting because it means that every day I can—and in fact, will!—make a difference. And it's frightening for the same reason, because the difference I make can be negative as well as positive. I can bring the kingdom of God closer to someone's life—perhaps even to a group of persons—by something I say, do, or write; and by the same token I can retard the kingdom by careless, self-centered, self-promoting activity. And of course I can be a deadweight on any kingdom prospect by simply doing nothing.

Fleming Rutledge put it powerfully in one of her sermons. "Cross-shaped acts of Christian courage, no matter how small, testify to the coming Day of the Lord, the ultimate triumph over evil."[1] "No matter how small": that word encourages me to know that my daily deeds are essential to the kingdom. But what kind of deeds? "Cross-shaped": now there's a description that can keep my soul on its knees each day. The kingdom of heaven is in unceasing conflict with the kingdoms of this world: our cross-shaped acts, small and routine and apparently insignificant as they may seem, are part of the process of heaven's "ultimate triumph over evil." This is wonderfully *daily* stuff. It may be small or large, but it is not ethereal or philosophical or theoretical; it is the stuff of eternity, lived out in hourly words and deeds.

And there's a holy contagion in all of this. Frederick Buechner suggests seeing humanity as "like an enormous spider web, so that if you touch it anywhere you set the whole thing trembling." Buechner refers to the far reach of the assassination of President John F. Kennedy, but then goes on to say that it need not be anything "so cataclysmic as the death of a president." "As we move around the world and as we act with kindness, perhaps, or with indifference, or with hostility, toward the people we meet, we too are setting the great spider web a-tremble. The life I touch for good or ill will touch another life, and that in turn another, until who knows where the trembling stops or in what far place my touch will be felt."[2]

I hope this thought strikes you as it does me—that it is both exciting and frightening. Buechner has been honest enough to remind us that our touch is potentially "for good or ill," and the corresponding and very far-reaching effect for one or the other. Which is to say, there are no little events in our universe. No one can estimate the reach of any particular deed or word. Some six centuries ago the French had a bit of peasant wisdom that George Herbert put in writing two centuries later: "For want of a nail the shoe is lost, for want of a shoe the horse is lost, for want of a horse the rider is lost." Some deed, some word—possibly insignificant in its own right—may just set a large portion of the web of humanity to quivering.

Our business, we kingdom-builders, is to employ the good. We can't be content to let the business of humanity rest on chance. If we believe God has a purpose in our world—indeed, that God has a vision of a kingdom for our world—then we must intentionally and positively involve ourselves in the process. Small or smaller, large or larger, each deed and each word can be a kingdom-action.

Sometimes the kingdom action is by countering evil. On occasions you and I find ourselves in social conversations where a racial, ethnic, or economic group is being maligned, or an individual is being victimized by gossip. Our natural tendency may be to acquiesce by our silence or perhaps even to join in on the dismantling. The web of destruction is shaking! It's a good time to speak a quiet, cautionary word—"perhaps there's more to the story than we know." Personally, I find myself in danger of imitating the character that I'm opposing, which is of course self-defeating. If I allow irresponsible comments to irritate me to the point where I become testy or sarcastic, I've become part of the problem rather than of the solution. Sometimes this countering of evil is at a very modest level—some would say an inconsequential one. Some work causes people to see themselves as very routine. The person restocking shelves at the grocery store or the officer examining luggage and passenger credentials at the airport can hardly be blamed if they fail to see us as persons, but you and I can help if we will see *them* as persons. No big show, mind you, no Lady Bountiful display, just a warm greeting or thank-you, and the person in a faceless job gets new life. Last week one of my favorite people told me of the rules he has given his college-age daughter as she evaluates the young men she dates. One of them: see how he treats the server at the restaurant. I confess that my regard for several religious leaders has gone down when I've seen their disregard for the people serving them. I don't know that the kingdom of God will come in by the vote of the servers and busboys' union, but I wouldn't rule out the possibility. After all, Jesus said that the kingdom of God is like a mustard seed. The kingdom starts as a little thing—and thus, I reason, in little ways.

A colleague told me why he always parks at a spot some distance from the building housing his office. One rainy morning he got the last parking place near the building, then saw the car following him go half a block away, where an office worker stepped from her car into a puddle of water, then picked her way through rain and rough terrain to the building. Ever since, he explained, he has parked at the farther lot. You may call me a sentimentalist and perhaps you'll be right, but I call that kingdom-living. It may not bring in the kingdom, but at least it won't get in the way.

One of my heroes in the middle of the twentieth century was Dag Hammarskjöld, Secretary General of the

United Nations. He strove to live out his life in imitation of Christ, convinced that, as he said, "In our era, the road to holiness necessarily passes through the world of action."[3] For Hammarskjöld the action was on a world stage, even to the point of his tragic death in a plane crash while on a peace-keeping mission in Africa. Few if any of us will have such a leading role, but the rule of action remains. Some of the action will come through the way we spend and give our money, and some of it through that neglected and undervalued action of prayer.

Most of the action will come through relationships with people. Now and again I may have a chance to lead a soul to faith in Christ, or to strengthen someone's faith by voice or note or prayer. Sometimes I will do it best simply by listening to someone's pain and crying with them—or hearing of someone's little victory and rejoicing with them.

But all of us have opportunity every day to cast our vote for the kingdom of heaven in ways large and small. And I dare to say that most of the time we won't know which votes are large ones and which small. But the opportunities are there—in our workplace and our social engagements, our telephone conversations and our Internet communication, with family and with strangers.

I find it tremendously exciting to think I will have a role today in bringing in the kingdom of God. How wonderful to be part of something so big! You and I have only one life on this planet, you know. My life won't seem much to a keeper of history, but it's all I have—and it's the only thing for which God will judge me. Therefore this life, with all its kingdom possibilities, is inestimably valuable to me. I want to be sure how I use it in touching the web of life, through my fellow occupants on planet earth.

I hope today to make a step toward bringing in the kingdom of God. And tomorrow, God willing, I hope to do the same. Isn't that exciting? Frederick Buechner calls it, "Life with a capital L." I say it's the only way to live.

NOTES

1. Fleming Rutledge, *The Undoing of Death* (Grand Rapids: William Eerdmans Publishers, 2002), 231-32.

2. Frederick Buechner, *Listening to Your Life* (New York: Harper SanFrancisco, 1992), 139.

3. "The Invisible Man," *Time*, 10-23-64, p. 110.

DISCUSSION GUIDE FOR *I BOUGHT A HOUSE ON GRATITUDE STREET*, BY J. ELLSWORTH KALAS

John D. Schroeder

CHAPTER 1
I BOUGHT A HOUSE ON GRATITUDE STREET

Snapshot Summary
This chapter explores the importance of gratitude for all God has given us. It looks at the roles humility, self-knowledge, and maturity play and how we can give back to others.

Reflection / Discussion Questions
1. What does it mean to live on Gratitude Street? What is needed in order to live there?

2. Respond to the author's statement that essentially everything we own is a gift.

3. Why is maturity important? How are maturity and defeats linked?

4. Why is it critical to admit our role in defeat and to stop looking for others to blame?

5. Reflect on / discuss the importance of self-knowledge and humility.

6. Share something another person has done to make your life better.

7. Why does deprivation often provide good soil for feelings of gratitude?

8. List some reasons we fail to be grateful.

9. What are some ways in which we can express our gratefulness to God and to others?

10. Share your own thoughts and experiences concerning gratitude and what you learned about gratitude from this chapter.

Prayer
Dear God, thank you for all you have given us. We are grateful to you for all your blessings. Help us be a blessing to others. Amen.

CHAPTER 2
KEEP CONFESSED UP

Snapshot Summary
This chapter looks at the benefits of regular confession, and why we need to acknowledge our shortcomings to God and others.

Reflection / Discussion Questions
1. Share a memorable lesson from your life that is related to confession.

2. What are some of the benefits of regular confession?

3. Reflect on / discuss how the Hebrews recognized the importance of confession.

4. What do you think confession should include? How often should you confess?

5. Reflect on / discuss Samuel Johnson's habit of confessing presented in this chapter.

6. Why do we need a Divine Listener for our confessions?

7. What can happen when we fail to confess our sins and shortcomings?

8. What often prevents people from regular confession? List some obstacles.

9. What does God promise if we confess our sins?

10. What did you learn about confession from reading this chapter?

Prayer
Dear God, thank you for listening to us at all times, especially when we confess our sins and shortcomings. And thank you for the forgiveness you offer to us for our failings. Amen.

CHAPTER 3
DON'T TAKE YOURSELF TOO SERIOUSLY

Snapshot Summary
This chapter uses the biblical story of Elijah to show why we need to keep our seriousness in balance and know our limitations.

Reflection / Discussion Questions
1. Reflect on / discuss the story of Elijah and what we can learn from it about taking things too seriously.

2. Share a time when you took something too seriously.

3. What are some of the possible consequences of being too serious?

4. Name some reasons we may take things too seriously.

5. What are some warning signs that you may be taking things too seriously?

6. Why is self-esteem important? In what ways does self-esteem have limits?

7. Describe some ways we can keep our seriousness in balance.

8. What does God want us to take seriously?

9. Reflect on / discuss why we are important to God and others.

10. Share your thoughts about human limitations and why we need to know our own limits.

Prayer

Dear God, thank you for loving us even when we take ourselves too seriously and dwell on our importance. Help us take seriously what is important to you and to others. Amen.

CHAPTER 4
INVEST IN GOOD MEMORIES

Snapshot Summary

This chapter examines the role that good memories play in our lives and why they are treasures and gifts from God.

Reflection / Discussion Questions

1. Share a favorite memory from your life.
2. Reflect on / discuss why memory is a special gift.
3. What type of memories would we all like to forget?
4. Explain how and why not all of our memories are of our own choosing.
5. What characteristics do most good memories share?
6. What does the Bible tell us about memories?
7. Reflect on / discuss how memories can play tricks on us.
8. How can we help our memories by giving them something to work with?
9. Describe some ways to invest in good memories.
10. Reflect on / discuss the importance of having a ritual of memory.

Prayer

Dear God, thank you for the gift of our memories. Thank you for the joy they bring us and the important role they play in our lives. Amen.

CHAPTER 5
MAKE FRIENDS OF YOUR REGRETS

Snapshot Summary
This chapter looks at regrets and guilt. It shows us how and why we should forgive ourselves, befriend regrets, and keep a healthy attitude about them.

Reflection / Discussion Questions
1. What is regret? Share your own definition of regret and give an example.
2. List some common regrets that many people possess.
3. How is regret like anger?
4. What are some of the hazards of making friends with your regrets?
5. What are some actions or non-actions that we should regret?
6. Why is it wise to befriend our regrets?
7. Reflect on / discuss some of the damage regrets can cause.
8. Name some healthy regrets.
9. What is the connection between regret and guilt?
10. Name some practical ways you can make friends with regret.

Prayer
Dear God, thank you for showing us how to productively deal with our regrets. Help us strive for a healthy attitude in all aspects of our lives. Amen.

CHAPTER 6
BE GLAD GOD KNOWS YOU SO WELL

Snapshot Summary
This chapter encourages us to enjoy and enhance our friendship with God.

Reflection / Discussion Questions

1. Why should we be glad God knows us so well?

2. Describe the benefits of having a friend who knows you well and who still likes you.

3. What does God often see in us that we don't see in ourselves?

4. How are friendships with people different from friendship with God?

5. What secrets and insights about friendship does Genesis reveal?

6. Why do we need this friendship with God? List some of the benefits.

7. Share a time when you needed and depended upon God's friendship.

8. How can we keep our friendship with God current and alive?

9. Reflect on / discuss how a growing friendship with God makes us better suited for human friendships.

10. What new insights about God and friendship did you receive from this chapter?

Prayer

Dear God, thank you for your continuous love and friendship with us, even in those times when we do not deserve it. We are glad you know us so well. Help us get to know you better. Amen.

CHAPTER 7
FALL IN LOVE WITH YOUR RAINY DAYS

Snapshot Summary

This chapter encourages us to embrace and even love the difficult times in our life.

Reflection / Discussion Questions

1. What does it mean to fall in love with rainy days?

2. Share a time when you experienced a rainy day.

3. How did the apostle Paul handle the difficult times and situations in his life?

4. What impresses you most about the apostle Paul?

5. How can prayer sustain us during the rainy days of life?

6. Explain why our circumstances have little to do with the will of God.

7. Name some creative ways to respond to and embrace rainy days.

8. Share a time when you experienced the faithfulness of God during or after a rainy day.

9. Why, according to the author, do we actually need rainy days? How do they help us?

10. What were some of the difficult times experienced by Jesus during his ministry?

Prayer

Dear God, thank you for life, the good and the bad days. Help us remember that you are always with us in the pouring rain, as well as when life is sunny. Amen.

CHAPTER 8
A FRIEND IS A FRIEND IS A FRIEND

Snapshot Summary

This chapter expands our vision of friendship with others and shows how we need all types of friends in our lives.

Reflection / Discussion Questions

1. In your own words, give a definition of a friend or friendship.

2. Share a time when a friend gave you needed support or encouragement.

3. Why do we need friends? Name some of the reasons.

4. Explain the statement that to be human is to have a variety of friends.

5. How does a close friend differ from a casual one? Why are both valuable?

6. Describe some situations or circumstances that strengthen friendships.

7. What lessons about friendship did you learn as a child?

8. Are adult friendships any different from those of children? Explain.

9. What can we learn about friendship from the life of King David?

10. Name some simple and practical ways we can be a friend to others.

Prayer
Dear God, thank you for the gift of friendships and for our friends who come in all shapes and sizes. Help us cherish our friends and strengthen our relationships with others. Amen.

CHAPTER 9
GET A GOOD NIGHT'S SLEEP

Snapshot Summary
This chapter explores the topic of sleep. It shows why sleep is important and why sleep is a gift from God, and it offers advice about getting good sleep.

Reflection / Discussion Questions
1. Describe how you feel after a good night's sleep.

2. What are some things that can prevent or disrupt sleep?

3. If you do not sleep well, how does it affect you and your day?

4. What are some common techniques people use to fall asleep?

5. Why can prayer help you fall asleep at night?

6. Reflect on / discuss the wisdom concerning sleep found in the Creation story.

7. What does Psalm 127:2 tell us about the connection between God and sleep?

8. Explain why sleep is a gift from God.

9. What role does faith play in our sleeping?

10. In what ways does God provide for us while we sleep?

Prayer
Dear God, thank you for the gift of sleep. Help us cherish it and use it often to refresh ourselves for better service to you and others. Amen.

CHAPTER 10
TEACH US TO NUMBER OUR DAYS

Snapshot Summary
This chapter reminds us to value and make the most of each day we are given to live. It also offers practical advice on how to live when our days are numbered.

Reflection / Discussion Questions
1. Reflect on / discuss the wisdom of numbering our days.

2. What impressed you about the story of the woman who was given a year to live?

3. What reminders does life give us that our days are numbered?

4. How can remembering that our days are numbered help us live a better life?

5. If you learned you had only one more year to live, what would you do?

6. Name some productive ways to number our remaining days.

7. Reflect on / discuss why the author and others place a high value on reading books.

8. What places would you like to see before you die?

9. How would you describe a day well spent?

10. What does God want us to do with our remaining time?

Prayer
Dear God, thank you for reminding us that our days are numbered. Help us make the most of each moment, day, week, and month in service to you and others. Amen.

CHAPTER 11
IF YOU CAN SEE IT, YOU CAN HAVE IT

Snapshot Summary
This chapter is about achieving our goals and dreams by seeing what we want, then going after it.

Reflection / Discussion Questions

1. Share something you have dreamed about or desired all your life.

2. What lessons can we learn from the story of Elijah and Elisha?

3. Reflect on / discuss the importance of having a passionate commitment to goals.

4. Name some reasons many people fail to reach their goals.

5. Why is seeing the first step toward achieving?

6. Reflect on / discuss the need for having a grand vision in life.

7. Name some of the multiple applications of the see-it, have-it principle.

8. Reflect on / discuss saintliness. Why is it rarely mentioned and rarely sought?

9. What goals do you think God wants us to achieve in life?

10. Share a new insight you gained from this chapter.

Prayer
Dear God, thank you for giving us the ability to reach our goals. Help us open our eyes to expand our vision, and help us achieve our dreams. Amen.

CHAPTER 12
BRING IN GOD'S KINGDOM EVERY DAY

Snapshot Summary
This chapter examines the kingdom of God, the role each of us plays in it, and how we can bring it to reality as kingdom-builders.

Reflection / Discussion Questions
1. What images come to mind when you think of the kingdom of God?

2. Reflect on / discuss what Jesus said during his ministry about the kingdom of God.

3. Why is there so much discussion and speculation about God's kingdom?

4. According to the author, what two things are clear about the kingdom?

5. Reflect on / discuss how each of us can participate in bringing in the kingdom of heaven.

6. Why are our daily deeds essential to the kingdom?

7. Reflect on / discuss what Frederick Buechner says about humanity and how we influence each other.

8. Give some examples of the effect our lives have upon others, both for good and for ill.

9. Reflect on / discuss the business of being a kingdom-builder.

10. Share some of the lessons you learned from reading this book and from your reflection or discussion.

Prayer
Dear God, thank you for encouraging us to bring in your kingdom each day. Remind us that we belong to you, and remind us to work for you. Amen.